The Country Journal Book of Hardy Trees and Shrubs

ILLUSTRATIONS BY ALLIANORA ROSSE

THE COUNTRY JOURNAL BOOK OF

HARDY TREES AND SHRUBS

BY HARRISON L. FLINT

Country Journal Publishing Company, Brattleboro, Vermont, 1983

Copyright © 1983 by Country Journal Publishing Co., Inc.
All rights reserved under International
and Pan-American Copyright Conventions.
Published in the United States by
Country Journal Publishing Company, Inc.
205 Main Street, Brattleboro, Vermont 05301

Distributed to the trade by W. W. Norton & Co., Inc.,
500 Fifth Avenue, New York, New York 10036

The map on page x is reprinted from
Fruits and Berries for the Home and Garden
by Lewis Hill. © 1977 by Lewis Hill.
Reproduced by permission of Alfred A. Knopf, Inc.

The Country Journal Book of Hardy Trees and Shrubs
was designed by Thomas Morley. The text was
composed on the Linotron 202 in Electra by Dix
Type Inc., Syracuse, New York. The book was
printed and bound by The Alpine Press, Inc.,
Stoughton, Massachusetts. The paper is 60-pound
Mohawk Vellum Satin. Production was supervised by
William Farnham. Copy editing was done by Barbara
Hewes. Ann Kearton was the art assistant.

Library of Congress Cataloguing in Publication Data

Flint, Harrison L. (Harrison Leigh), 1929–
   The Country journal book of hardy trees and shrubs.

  Bibliography: p. 157
  Includes index.
  1. Ornamental trees—United States. 2. Ornamental
shrubs—United States. 3. Landscape gardening—United
States. 4. Ornamental trees—Canada. 5. Ornamental
shrubs—Canada. 6. Landscape gardening—Canada.
I. Blair & Ketchum's country journal. II. Title.
III. Title: Hardy trees and shrubs.
SB435.5.F54   1983   635.9′77′0973   82-19914

Manufactured in the United States of America

First Edition

ISBN 0-918678-02-1

10 9 8 7 6 5 4 3 2 1

To my mother

Contents

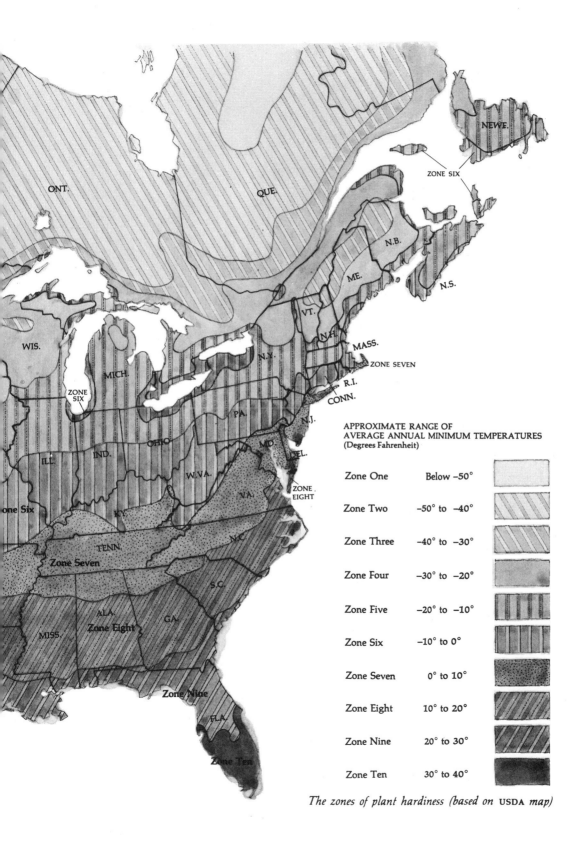

APPROXIMATE RANGE OF
AVERAGE ANNUAL MINIMUM TEMPERATURES
(Degrees Fahrenheit)

Zone One	Below −50°	
Zone Two	−50° to −40°	
Zone Three	−40° to −30°	
Zone Four	−30° to −20°	
Zone Five	−20° to −10°	
Zone Six	−10° to 0°	
Zone Seven	0° to 10°	
Zone Eight	10° to 20°	
Zone Nine	20° to 30°	
Zone Ten	30° to 40°	

The zones of plant hardiness (based on USDA *map)*

INTRODUCTION

LANDSCAPE PLANTS ENRICH LIFE in many ways. They provide comfort by protecting us and our dwellings from winter wind and summer sun. They add beauty to our surroundings by their color, form, texture, and seasonal changes. Properly placed, they define space, affording privacy and making the outdoors as useful as the indoors. They may even serve primal needs for feelings of protection and enclosure.

Plants add much more than their original cost and upkeep to the value of properties. In contrast with most other things we buy, their value appreciates rather than depreciates with age. Used properly they are a good investment, at the same time contributing much to the physical and aesthetic quality of our lives.

Cold climates present special challenges to landscape gardeners in selecting trees and shrubs for landscape use. Residents of northern areas have found, often by bitter experience, that all the other good qualities in the world are of no avail if the plant chosen cannot survive the winter. Yet we cannot lose sight of those other qualities in our quest for cold-hardy landscape plants.

Choosing the right plant for a specific landscape need is not a simple task. There are many factors to be considered, but they are all included in these five questions:

(1) Is the plant adaptable to the climate of the region and the soil and microclimate of the planting site?

(2) How is it expected to function, and will its mature size, form, and texture allow it to do this?

(3) Does it need any special care, and am I prepared to give it or pay professionals to do so?

(4) How aesthetically appealing is it, and at what seasons of the year?

(5) Is it available, and how expensive is it to buy, plant, and maintain?

The ability of a plant to succeed in a given site depends upon characteristics of both plant and site. Tolerance of high and low temperatures, sun and shade, wet and dry soil, and degree of soil acidity can all be important.

In cold climates, winter-hardiness most often limits adaptability. This includes tolerance of outright cold, winter desiccation, wind, roadside salt, and even the mechanical stress of ice and snow. Even though winter-hardiness includes several components, the one that most often determines the usefulness of a plant in a given site is its tolerance of extreme cold. This is why we use hardiness-zone maps and plant designations. Hardiness zones are areas that experience similar cold extremes, usually measured as *average annual minimum temperature*. The map on pages x and xi, adapted from one prepared by the U.S. Department of Agriculture (USDA Miscellaneous Publication 814), divides the United States and southern Canada into numbered zones 10°F wide. Plants may be rated by this system. Sugar maple *(Acer saccharum)*, for example, is considered cold-hardy in northern areas with an average annual minimum temperature of −30°F to −40°F; thus it can be expected to be hardy in Zone 3 and milder zones. In addition to the USDA map, other plant hardiness-zone maps are in use. Since different maps use different numbering systems, it is important to use maps and plant designations based on the same system. Actual temperature ranges are used in this book.

Adaptability of plants depends not only on the cold extremes of the general area where they are located but also on the microclimate of the particular site. The south side of a building, for example, provides a distinctly different microclimate from the north side. Such differences provide opportunities to use specific plants, as well as imposing limitations to their use. For example, broadleaved evergreens such as mountain andromeda *(Pieris floribunda)* and some rhododendrons may be damaged by fluctuating temperatures and drying if planted with a southern or western exposure, but come through well in the more uniform temperatures and winter shade provided by a northern exposure.

Soil conditions can be as important as climate in limiting adaptability of plants. Some trees and shrubs, such as red maple *(Acer rubrum)* and red osier dogwood *(Cornus sericea)*, grow well in poorly drained soils, but the majority of plants do not. Plants also vary widely in tolerance of dry soil and roadside salt.

So-called acid-soil plants, mostly members of the Heath family (Ericaceae), grow best in acidic soil (pH 4.5 to 5.5 or thereabouts). Many failures of rhododendrons and azaleas are the result of insufficiently acidic soil rather than the rigors of climate. This family also includes

2

blueberries, mountain andromeda, mountain-laurel, heathers, and
others. Most, but not all, members of this family grow best in peaty,
well-drained soil.

PLANT FUNCTION

It is always a good idea to know how a plant is to function before
selecting it. Some plants are chosen simply for the beauty that they will
add, but most will be needed for specific uses: shrubs or vines for visual
screening, ground covers for slopes or awkward corners where lawn
cannot be maintained easily, trees for shade and overhead enclosure.

To prepare for selection of landscape plants, have a plan in mind.
This may be no more than an image in the mind's eye when a small
corner is to be planted, or it may be a drawn landscape plan when an
entire property is to be landscaped. The important thing is that there
be some kind of plan. To subject oneself to the temptations of a garden
center without some plan is a little like jousting without armor, leaving
one susceptible to injury (or impulse buying).

Function dictates size limitations, and plants that will grow too large
for their space are a source of trouble forever. Be as realistic as possible
and do not overplant, either in size or numbers. Things may look a bit
sparse for the first two or three years, but eventually you will be glad of
your restraint.

MAINTENANCE

The price of a plant may seem high at the time you buy it, but be sure
that it will soon be exceeded by the cost of caring for it. Some plants
require relatively little maintenance, but all need some care, even if
only weeding. Careful landscape planning and selection of plants needing little care can minimize the cost and frustration that are inherent
in maintenance. Of course, there are some high-maintenance plants
with so much appeal that we will use them in spite of the trouble, but
there is a big difference between doing this and being caught unaware.

SEASONAL INTEREST

The aesthetic quality of a plant usually has many dimensions. Color—
of flowers, foliage, fruits, bark, and twigs—is the most obvious. Plant
form, branching patterns, and foliage texture also contribute.

If one considers plants to be (in one role) architectural materials, one
way in which they differ from other architectural materials is their
seasonal change. We value evergreens for their winter interest. Yet
taken alone evergreens can be monotonous. The fullest seasonal interest comes from variety and change.

Some plants are so spectacular for two weeks of the year that they
need not offer much interest the other fifty weeks to justify their inclu-

ST. JOHNSWORTS   FLOWERING CRABAPPLES

CREEPING JUNIPERS   SUMMERSWEET   SUGAR MAPLE

SWEET AUTUMN CLEMATIS   RUGOSA ROSE   AMERICAN HORNBEAM

The organization of plants in this book is by size—that is, from small to large, from vines and climbers that require some form of support, and low ground-cover plants, all the way to large shade trees that grow fifty feet tall or more. In Chapters I through VIII deciduous plants are discussed, in the order suggested by the drawing above. In Chapter IX a variety of evergreens are described.

AMERICAN ARBORVITAE   EASTERN WHITE PINE   MUGHO PINE

     CANADA HEMLOCK   FIRS   NORWAY SPRUCE

     CATAWBA RHODODENDRON   MOUNTAIN ANDROMEDA   YEWS

sion in the landscape. Others are never spectacular but remain quietly interesting for much or all of the year. To appreciate a plant's full potential, consider the full spectrum of its seasonal interest.

AVAILABILITY AND COST

Availability of landscape plants is constantly changing as managers of nurseries and garden centers try to maintain a balance between supply and future demand. Which plants become more available, and which less, depends on public demand, specifications of landscape designers, problems of production and supply, and promotion and advertising. Plants are continually entering the market, leaving, and re-entering. Consequently, availability of plants is only partly predictable.

If a plant is not available at one time or place, chances are it is available somewhere else, or will be a year or two later. The inconvenience of checking other sources, or waiting for a year, will be compensated for when the plant finally turns up. When there is no time for this, substitutes will often function well if they are selected carefully.

Fortunately, the sixty trees, shrubs, vines, and ground covers (and their cultivars, or horticultural varieties) that follow are by no means an all-inclusive list. They are some of the best plants for cold climates, but there are many others as well. Local nurseries, landscapers, extension agents, and knowledgeable amateurs can suggest substitutes well suited for landscape use in their locality.

PLANT NAMES

Common or vernacular names of plants vary from country to country and even regionally within countries. Unlike scientific names, they are not arbitrated by scientific bodies, so technically there are no "correct" or "incorrect" common names. Because these common names are the only names that a great many people know, they are important even though imprecise.

Scientific names are written in Latin, since that language is unchanging and is known (to varying degrees) throughout the international scientific community. Scientific classification actually consists of two names: the *genus* (plural *genera*), describing the kind of plant; and the *species* (plural also *species*), referring to the specific type within the genus. For example, sugar maple belongs to *Acer*, the genus of maples, and the species *saccharum*; thus *Acer saccharum*.

Cultivars, or cultivated varieties, are horticultural forms selected from wild species or produced through hybridization. Cultivars of landscape species are mostly clones, but may be purebreeding seed lines or F_1 hybrids. Their names are usually in the vernacular, but a few older ones are Latinized, and they are initially capitalized and enclosed in single quotation marks. Like scientific names, they are regulated by international agreement.

6

Validity of scientific names is arbitrated by international scientific bodies. At least in principle, there is international agreement as to which is the correct name for a plant, and names that have been incorrectly applied are called *synonyms*. Such names are not considered valid, yet frequently they still appear in nursery catalogs.

To be reasonably sure of obtaining the plant asked for, it is a good idea to use the scientific name as well as the common name. Most nursery and garden center operators are familiar with scientific names and use them in ordering plants from wholesale nurseries. Plants for sale are usually, but not universally, labelled with both their scientific and common names.

PLANNING FOR PLANTING

SELECTION AND PLANTING of trees and shrubs calls for preparation, in the form of some kind of plan. It is a mistake, however, to think of a landscape plan only as a means of deciding what plants to use and where to place them. Its usefulness goes far beyond that.

Landscape planning is a way of deciding how to use outdoor *space*, to provide maximum usefulness and pleasure for the humans who use that space. Selection and positioning of plants is not the first consideration. In fact, it comes well down the list, after locating buildings on the property, dealing with vehicular and pedestrian traffic, and deciding how the remaining outdoor space is to be used.

Who should do the landscape plan? In most areas there are landscape architects and other professionals qualified to carry out at least some aspects of landscape planning. When it comes to situating buildings, designing drives and walks, modifying earth forms, and providing for drainage, it may be required by building codes to leave these steps to the professionals. Usually it makes sense to let the landscape designer go a step further and identify areas in the landscape by intended use, and perhaps even prepare a planting plan.

Rather than having the opportunity to start from scratch, most people today find themselves with an existing home, in an existing landscape. Even then it may be a good idea to consult a landscape architect about drainage, drives, and walks—perhaps even a full plan. But those with enough interest in the subject can do their own planning. Here is how.

PLANNING YOUR OWN LANDSCAPE

If you decide to do it yourself, you will still need to have a plan on paper:

1. Start with an accurate scale drawing of your lot, showing all build-

8

ings and drives. Your town or county clerk may be able to help, but you may have to draw your own plan from your deed, or by measuring from your property lines as you know them. The important thing is that the plan should reflect as closely as possible what is really out there on the ground.

2. Label the rooms on the house plan. Think about the function of each. Then look at the yard areas outside and start asking yourself the kinds of questions that a landscape architect would ask: Does the indoor living area have direct access to the outside? If so, do you want an outdoor living area, for eating, relaxing, and playing, adjacent to the indoor living area? Where are the house's utility areas? How can they be most simply connected with the drive and for access to utilities and garbage disposal? What recreational areas are needed? If there are children in the family, how can they enter the house easily, with minimum disruption from muddy feet? Is there to be a vegetable garden? Will it be enough of a model garden (no weeds, neat rows) to be part of the outdoor living area? Or will it be more realistic to make it part of the utility area, screened from general view with fence or plantings? Think about all of the outdoor activities of every member of the family, and analyze them in this way.

3. Mark off your yard into three principal areas:

The *public area* probably will be the front yard, but perhaps only part of it, where visitors enter. It can present an attractive picture to passers-by and a feeling of welcome to visitors.

The *service area* is reserved for all the essential, but not always attractive, utilitarian activities around the home. As much as possible, gather them together and visually screen them from other areas.

The *private area* is for private and family activities such as relaxation and recreation, outdoor meals, sunbathing, and hobby gardening. It allows these activities to be carried on with as much privacy as desired, with the help of visual screening.

4. On paper, extend the borders of these areas into the house plan where it seems appropriate, to show indoor-outdoor relationships. Then subdivide the outdoor areas as necessary to accommodate specific activities, still keeping the plan as simple as possible. It should be possible to walk from one area to another easily and directly. Think about heavy foot-traffic areas, and plan simple walks where they are needed. Think about areas where plantings (or structures) are needed to enclose areas:

Ceiling Are shade trees needed? What about small patio trees to give a feeling of overhead enclosure as well as shade to outdoor sitting areas?

Walls Where are plants or fences needed to separate areas from each other and give privacy? Where should they be avoided or kept low to retain a view? Remember, shrubs usually are less costly for screening than fences if you start with small plants. But also think about the

9

waiting time for them to become large enough to function, and the ground space they will occupy. Also, solid fences and evergreen shrubs will screen year-round. Deciduous shrubs or vines on see-through fences will screen only during the leafy season. Decide whether that is enough.

Floor Lawn and walks may cover most of the outdoor "floor" space, but consider also mulch and ground cover plants at least for those awkward spaces that would be difficult to maintain any other way.

5. Don't worry about all the details of planting at first. If you are satisfied with the way you have divided the major functional areas, and you have decided where trees and screening shrubs or fences are needed, you will have come a long way—on paper. You can transform the plan into reality at your leisure, making minor adjustments as you go.

If all this whets your appetite and you want to learn more about landscape design, a good place to start is your public library. If you are close enough to a state university or horticultural society you may find more complete information in libraries there.

Don't forget about magazines and newspapers, especially those that carry garden and landscape information prepared by local and regional authorities rather than just syndicated stores from distant sources. Last but not least, remember to check with your local Cooperative Extension Service office, an invaluable source of reliable local information.

PLANTING AND CARE OF TREES AND SHRUBS

Nothing is more important for success in planting than timing. Commercial landscapers sometimes claim to be able to plant at almost any time of year, and this is true if one has the right equipment and is willing to absorb a few losses in the process. For most of us, it makes a lot more sense to go with nature's cycles and plant at the best possible time. When this is done, plants return to rapid growth soon, with minimal interruption from transplanting shock.

Spring is the preferred planting season for most bare-root trees and shrubs in cold climates. Trees with heavy sap flow, such as birches and sugar maple, are best transplanted as soon as the ground is workable in the spring. If it is necessary to delay until late spring, delay still further —until fall. Fleshy rooted trees such as magnolias, however, seem to recover best when planted in midspring, after the ground has warmed slightly.

Most evergreens are best planted as soon as summer's heat is over but before the leaves of deciduous trees fall—September in most northern areas. This allows several weeks for recovery before the soil becomes too cold for root growth. Evergreens planted too late for development of new roots before winter are unusually susceptible to winterburn of foliage, in some winters severe enough to kill newly planted evergreens. When it is not possible to plant in early autumn, wait until the following spring, the second-best time for transplanting evergreens.

Larger trees, evergreens, and some deciduous shrubs are available with a burlap-wrapped soil ball around the roots. Timing may be slightly less critical for these plants than for bare-root trees and shrubs, but is still important for best results.

11

Timing is less important for container-grown landscape plants, since few roots are lost at transplanting. These can be planted virtually anytime, but benefit from planting in spring or early summer to allow a long period for regrowth of roots before autumn.

When the timing has been worked out, be sure to make the planting hole more than large enough to accommodate the roots, spread in a natural position if bare-root. Mix organic matter and super- or treble-phosphate into the planting soil and have everything ready to receive the plants before they arrive. This will minimize the length of time the roots are out of the ground, an important factor in transplanting success.

Plant trees and shrubs at the same depth at which they were growing previously. When the hole is filled in, leave the soil surface slightly concave, with a ring or dam of extra soil around the edge to hold water until it soaks through to the roots. Water thoroughly after planting and be sure to add enough to penetrate the full depth of the root zone. Do not water again for at least a week or two, and then re-water at two to three week intervals, but only when the soil is clearly dry an inch or two below the surface.

Do not add fertilizer, other than phosphate and organic matter mixed into the planting hole, for at least half a growing season after planting. A mulch of wood chips, bark, or other available material can be added immediately after planting.

Transplanting Wild Seedlings

Many people in rural areas have successfully transplanted wild seedlings, yet the practice is seldom recommended. With most trees and shrubs, this requires careful timing and skillful aftercare, and even then success is chancy. I have seen sugar maples transplanted from the wild still alive but with practically no further growth fifteen years later. There are exceptions to this, but better results usually are obtained by using nursery-grown plants.

Another consideration in using wild plants is conservation. Some of the choicest wild plants are no longer commonly found and may become endangered before many years, if they are not already, especially when removed by overzealous gardeners and plant collectors. Most wild plant species are also propagated in nurseries for landscape use, without wiping out native stands, and such plants are easier to establish in the landscape.

Watering and Mulching

Once a tree or shrub has been planted in good soil for a year or two, it should rarely if ever need to be irrigated. It is possible, though, to hasten a tree's growth to functional size by watering it every week or two during dry weather. When a tree has become adapted to such intensive care, it cannot be suddenly stopped without risking damage. Rather, watering should be tapered off gradually over a couple of growing seasons.

Mulching to conserve moisture in the ground is a far better alternative to frequent irrigation, partly because mulches do so much else. They make it difficult for weed seedlings to get started. They keep the soil cool and moist in summer, and reduce temperature fluctuations all through the year. Finally, they can be attractive, enhancing the beauty of the landscape.

LIMING AND FERTILIZATION

In acidic soils, turfgrasses usually need to be limed, but most trees and shrubs do not. In fact, several landscape plants in the Heath Family (Ericaceae) *require* acidic soil for best growth. The rule with lime is—when in doubt, leave it out—for trees and shrubs, that is. If they should need a little lime they will probably get it by accident when the lawn is limed.

Fertilization of trees and shrubs is sometimes necessary, but in general it is a highly overrated practice. Adding phosphate to planting soil is usually a good idea, to promote new root growth. Phosphate moves incredibly slowly in soil, and the only practical way to get it to new roots is to place it there.

Once trees and shrubs are established, the only fertilizer element that they consistently respond to is nitrogen. Available forms of this element move quickly, sometimes too quickly, through the soil. We used to recommend stuffing a fertilizer mixture into the soil through channels made by auger or crowbar. This practice has been rightly called into question. It may be great exercise for otherwise sedentary humans, but it uses a lot of energy doing what gravity and a soaking rain do so effortlessly. Except for the therapeutic value, it probably is better to apply nitrogen fertilizer to the soil surface and wait for it to soak in.

Probably the most important consideration in fertilizing trees and shrubs is to decide whether it is really necessary. If not, don't do it. Maintaining vigor in older trees, to reduce susceptibility to disease, is a special case, but in many other situations fertilization may be hard to justify.

PRUNING

A famous horticulturist in the early years of this century is said to have stated that the best time to prune is "when the knife is sharp." There is considerable truth in this whimsical observation, but it needs a corollary: The best time to prune is when you have thought of a really good reason for doing so. Otherwise, forget it. The damage done every year by unnecessary pruning is staggering.

13

Pruning of trees can be justified early in life, to assist in forming a sound scaffold of branches to carry the weight of the full-grown tree. Once a landscape tree is well underway, the benefits of further pruning, other than to remove dead and diseased branches, may not justify the cost. On the other hand, the spread of Dutch elm disease has been slowed by a careful program of pruning and sanitation in many localities. Deciding when and how to prune trees is an important value judgment and should be done after getting the best advice possible.

One particularly offensive kind of tree pruning is stag-heading, or cutting off all the branches of a tree, allegedly to be sure they can't fall off in a storm and destroy roofs of nearby homes. The immediate logic of this is inescapable, but unfortunately such drastic pruning encourages rapid regrowth of wood softer than the original, creating in a few years a far greater hazard to life, limb, and shingles than the untouched original tree would have.

When pruning formal hedges, sometimes thought of as an art form, also consider one simple scientific principle. If the hedge is wider at the top than below, the lower parts will be shaded by the canopy-like top, and decline. However else a hedge is pruned, it is important that it be kept wider at the base than at the top for uniform exposure to sun. Maintaining a good hedge is difficult if we forget this principle, but surprisingly easy if we make use of it.

Formal hedges may also need light applications of fertilizer annually to maintain vigor, and irrigation during drought. They may need to be pruned two or three times a year if made up of fast-growing deciduous shrubs, or only once annually, in early summer, if made up of evergreens such as hemlock or yew. Hedges are high-maintenance plantings, and should always be recognized as such.

There are several approaches to pruning deciduous shrubs. Perhaps the most common approach is not to prune at all. Next, in order of simplicity, is to cut an entire shrub to within a few inches of the ground. Drastic renovation, as this is sometimes called, can be lethal when used on the wrong plant. But for fast-growing shrubs such as privets, forsythia, beautybush (*Kolkwitzia*), and some viburnums, there is something to be said for the simplicity of this method.

A more traditional method is to remove about one third of the old branches each year and cut back the tips of the remaining stems to promote branching-out. This takes more time, but when skillfully done it never leaves the plant unsightly. Whether shrubs are to be renewed drastically or gradually, the time to do it is spring or early summer at the latest.

Evergreens can be ruined by unnecessary pruning even more easily than deciduous trees and shrubs. When in doubt, it is better to leave conifers alone than to risk permanent damage. But sometimes pruning is necessary. A prime example is the Japanese yew—a tree in Japan but seldom used as such here. If we use it in the upright form as a tree, we needn't prune it. As a shrub it will need some pruning eventually. The trick is to do it so that the basic plant form is retained, rather than turn perfectly good evergreen shrubs into globes, cylinders, cones, and blobs. To do this, cut away outer ends of branches *individually*, preserving the informal, graceful appearance of the plant.

Pines and spruces sometimes are pruned for fullness when used as visual screens. These trees must be pruned at exactly the right time and in exactly the right way. Consult directions for landscapers and Christmas-tree growers, available from most Cooperative Extension Service offices.

Pruning is an art as well as a science. Perhaps the greatest art is that of restraint—learning when not to prune. Pruning can be simultaneously therapeutic for the pruner and damaging to the plant. Bear both sides of the question in mind and, whenever possible, prune only with a purpose.

PEST CONTROL

The variety of pesticides and our awareness of the consequences of their misuse both have grown rapidly since the early 1960s. We now know that we cannot, either safely or legally, apply such chemicals casually.

Pest control has become increasingly the province of trained and licensed pesticide operators, including arborists and landscape contractors, but some pesticide applications still can be made by informed amateurs. To find out what you can and cannot do, consult your county Cooperative Extension Service office.

When you are ready to proceed, read *all* the information on the pesticide label and take *all* the recommended precautions.

From the start, remember that there are other ways of controlling many plant pests. Follow good sanitation practices: remove and burn deadwood and plant litter from diseased or infested plants. Control weeds by mulching and by placing plants so as to cover as much bare ground as possible in keeping with good planting design.

Finally, select landscape plants that are resistant to most of these problems. The result will be less time and money spent in controlling insects, diseases, and weeds, and more available for enjoying your landscape.

VINES AND CLIMBERS, NEEDING SUPPORT I

VINES AND CLIMBERS are would-be trees or shrubs that cannot support themselves. How tall they grow and how well they function depend more on the support provided than on their own growth habits.

Supporting structures or objects must be high enough to carry a vine to the height required, and strong enough to support it as it increases in mass. If sweet autumn clematis is to be used for visual screening on a chain-link fence, for example, it seems obvious that the top of the fence must be above eye level for the vine to reach that height. It may not be so obvious that a fine latticework trellis that would support clematis might be pulled to pieces by the tremendous weight of a mature bittersweet vine.

Vines can damage their support in other ways than just by their weight. Those that cling by aerial rootlets, such as English ivy and climbing hydrangea, or by adhesive tendrils, such as Boston ivy and Virginia creeper, can damage wooden clapboards and shingles, partly by direct penetration and partly by hindering air circulation and encouraging mildew and wood-rotting fungi underneath the foliage canopy.

These same vines can hasten crumbling of mortar in masonry walls. Before allowing such vines to climb, check the condition of the mortar and re-point if necessary. Established vines may eventually need to be cut back and pulled from the wall to clear the wall for repairs. Do this in late spring or early summer and the vine will begin to come back in the same growing season, returning to full function in two or three years.

To determine what kind of support a vine should be given, consider how it climbs and holds. Some, such as bittersweet and wisteria, climb vigorously by twining stems, and should be kept away from young trees, since they can literally grow over a young sapling and eventually kill it. Clematis, with twining leaf petioles rather than stems, climbs wire mesh and fine latticework well but is hopeless on walls and tree trunks unless additional wire support is provided.

Vines with tendrils, such as Virginia creeper, hold well to wire fence and rough tree bark, and forms with adhesive discs at the ends of tendrils also hold firmly to solid walls.

The few vines that follow are among the most functional and reliable for cold climates. They can be supplemented by others, such as Jackman clematis, Dutchman's pipe (*Aristolochia durior*), Dropmore Scarlet vine honeysuckle, and silver fleece vine (*Polygonum aubertii*).

Bittersweet

IN THE NORTH COUNTRY, where summer is short and spring almost nonexistent in some years, landscape plants with autumn and winter interest are especially appreciated. One of the best of these is American bittersweet (*Celastrus scandens*), a native twining vine with an unusually wide natural distribution: from Quebec to North Carolina and westward to South Dakota and New Mexico.

Even though bittersweet is most colorful in autumn and winter, it is also handsome in summer, with a dense mass of lustrous, deep green foliage that makes an effective visual screen. Since this vine climbs and supports itself by its twining stems, it needs something to twine around, such as latticework or chain-link fence. Buildings and large trees offer little for the stems to hold to, but bittersweet can quickly climb into the branches of small trees, eventually killing them by girdling or by blocking sunlight; so keep it away from saplings. This vine grows so rapidly and becomes so heavy that any trellis provided for it must be of heavy construction, built with 2- by 2-inch lumber at least.

Flowers of bittersweet are small and inconspicuous as they open in early summer. By late summer the fruiting capsules have begun to turn yellow, and by early autumn they are fully colored and breaking open to expose three cells, each with a seed or two covered with a bright red

18

outer coating. This combination of red and golden yellow accompanies the bright yellow autumn foliage until it falls, and then keeps the plant colorful until midwinter.

Not all bittersweet vines fruit well. The plant is nearly dioecious (having flowers of only one sex on an individual specimen). Female plants frequently bear a few male flowers, but there are not always enough to provide for adequate pollination and complete setting of fruit. Plants of known sex are sometimes available in nurseries, and it is a good idea to include a male plant in any group to insure a good supply of pollen.

An added attraction of bittersweet is that fruiting branches can be cut in fall and winter for indoor decorations without damaging the plant. In fact, a mature plant may need further pruning even after fruiting branches have been cut for all the neighbors.

Rapid growth can be a liability as well as an asset. It should be obvious by now that a bittersweet vine needs plenty of space. If only a small area is available, it is better to plant something else than to wage an annual battle to keep this rank-growing vine under control.

Bittersweet grows wild in northern areas where annual minimum temperatures average − 30°F or lower, so it is perfectly hardy anywhere in the northeastern and midwestern United States. It grows best with full exposure to sun and thrives in almost any soil that is not exceptionally wet or dry. In good soils, it usually is trouble free, but when euonymus scale insects become troublesome, they must be controlled in order to save the plant. This problem is less serious in the coldest climates than it is farther south.

Oriental bittersweet (*Celastrus orbiculata*) from China and Japan, a close relative of American bittersweet, is about as common in nurseries as the American native. Although it is less cold-hardy (it is not reliable in areas where annual winter minimum temperatures average below − 20°F), it can be considered equivalent in landscape effect. The two species are easily distinguished when in flower or fruit: the flowers of American bittersweet are generally located at the ends of branches; those of Oriental bittersweet generally form along the sides of branches in the axils of leaves.

Bittersweet can be obtained from some, but not all, nurseries. It is rather easy to propagate from established plants by rooting softwood cuttings in early summer. Place them in sand, soak thoroughly, cover with a tent of clear, tightly-sealed polyethylene film, and shade from direct sun. After the cuttings are well rooted, remove the plastic gradually and then transplant in a lightly shaded bed. Leave the cuttings in place, watering during dry periods, until the following spring, when they can be moved to a permanent location. Whether plants are newly propagated or nursery-grown, they will grow rapidly when established and should give years of autumn and winter color.

19

Sweet Autumn Clematis

AUTUMN IS A HIGHLY REGARDED SEASON in the North, with many natural attractions: crisp air, colorful trees, and a myriad of fascinating roadside plants. Among the most interesting plants in early autumn's roadside scene are the fragrant-flowered fall-blooming clematis vines. And these same plants can be valuable elements in the man-made landscape as well.

Our native virgin's-bower clematis (*Clematis virginiana*) grows wild through most of the Northeast. Its European relative, traveler's joy (*Clematis vitalba*), has larger flowers and grows more vigorously. But the most ornamental of all the fall-flowering clematis is an Asian species, sweet autumn clematis (*Clematis paniculata*, or—to be technically correct—*Clematis maximowicziana*). This vine is the most vigorous of the group, and has the best foliage, remaining dark green well into late autumn. Its flowers are not large in comparison with those of the large-flowering clematis hybrids, but they appear in tremendous profusion and scent the air over a wide area.

This Japanese native has been cultivated in the Northeast for more than 100 years, occasionally escaping to the wild here. Frank Conkling Seymour's *The Flora of New England* (Charles E. Tuttle Company, Rutland, Vermont, 1969) documents its return to the wild in Vermont, Massachusetts, Rhode Island, and Connecticut, attesting to its wide adaptability to the region. Its hardiness in the very coldest parts of New England has not been recorded, but it is known to tolerate climates with occasional cold snaps to −25°F. Like many other clematis, it can be killed to the ground in an especially severe winter, yet return with vigor and profuse flowering in a single growing season. If it should not prove hardy enough for the occasional −40°F cold of New England's

20

most severe climates, a substitute is the admittedly less vigorous and showy native virgin's-bower clematis.

Functionally, clematis is useful primarily for visual screening where proper support is available. Sweet autumn clematis is especially effective used in this way, and makes a dense mass of foliage from late spring through late autumn. Since it climbs by twining its petioles (leaf stalks) around any slender supporting structure, it cannot support itself on a wall, tree trunk, or heavy-membered trellis unless wires or strings are attached. It is ideally suited for climbing on chain-link fence, a characteristic that gives this outstanding countryside plant a functional use in the city.

Sweet autumn clematis, as well as the large-flowered clematis hybrids, grows best in well-drained, limey soils of reasonably good fertility. Gardeners sometimes have difficulty getting hybrid clematis varieties established and growing well, but sweet autumn clematis is relatively easy to start. First, the soil should be prepared as deeply as possible. English gardeners have long recommended digging planting holes 3 feet or more in depth—an amusing thought to many gardeners on New England's shallow soils. Nevertheless, deep soil preparation encourages roots to grow deeply, and this accomplishes two things: plants are less vulnerable to occasional drought, and the root zone remains cool even in midsummer, favoring strong summer growth.

If the soil is acidic, as most New England soils tend to be, ground limestone should be mixed with the planting soil. A good trial rate is 2 ounces of ground limestone mixed thoroughly into each bushel of planting soil, but a more accurate rate can be determined by having the soil tested for its lime requirement.

Liberal use of organic matter, such as compost, cow manure, or peat moss, in the planting soil usually is of great benefit. Along with organic matter, add superphosphate in about the same quantity as the ground limestone, or treblephosphate in about half the quantity. If peat moss is added, more ground limestone may be needed, as most peat moss makes the soil more acidic. For example, if peat moss to one fourth of the volume is mixed with the soil, the lime requirement may be as much as twice the amount that would have been needed without the peat moss.

Except for the materials already mentioned, fertilization should not be necessary for a year after planting if compost or manure is used. If peat moss is used instead, and growth is vigorous by midsummer, make a light application of complete garden fertilizer then. Otherwise, complete fertilizer, at recommended garden rates, can be applied annually, in the spring.

Sweet autumn clematis is widely available at many retail nurseries and some mail-order nurseries. Since it is a fence-grower, it might be considered as a cooperative planting project between neighbors.

21

Virginia Creeper

ONLY A FEW WOODY VINES can be grown in far northern areas. One of the hardiest and most versatile of these is a native, and so common as to be easily overlooked. Virginia creeper (*Parthenocissus quinquefolia*), also called woodbine, grows wild through most of the northeastern states, westward to Missouri, and southward all the way to Mexico. It is handsome and durable and a useful addition to many landscapes.

The leaves of Virginia creeper are distinctively compound, usually of five leaflets, palmately arranged (all attached at a single point). In the wild this plant grows as a vine, scrambling over the ground and climbing tree trunks in its path, much like its relatives the grapes.

Virginia creeper is winter-hardy in the coldest parts of the Northeast, assuming native northern material is used. In landscape use, as in the wild, it grows in full sun or deep shade and in moist to dry soil, but it does best in moderately moist soil, in full or partial sun.

This landscape plant is most interesting when it is in leaf, from late spring through midautumn. Foliage emerges light green, quickly maturing to a deep green, with a distinctively coarse texture. In early autumn, when the leaves of most plants are still green, those of the Virginia creeper in full sun turn brilliant red. In midautumn, as other plants are reaching peak color, the leaflets of Virginia creeper begin to fall, leaving leaf stalks attached for a while longer. After all the foliage has fallen, quiet landscape interest is maintained for a few more weeks by the small fruits, which resemble wild grapes.

In landscape use, Virginia creeper is at its best in naturalized situations, functioning as if in the wild, scrambling over irregular, rock-strewn ground, banks, and stone walls. It is aggressive, covering large areas quickly, but it is easily contained with occasional pruning. Since it does not climb by twining, it does not become hopelessly entangled in shrub and tree branches. And when it climbs trees, its tendrils hold firmly by entering crevices in the bark, but without harming the trees.

Virginia creeper is frequently recommended as a bank cover, and functions well in this role when the bank is not excessively steep nor the soil too dry. Under ideal conditions, it will root down as it spreads, with some stabilizing effect on mild slopes. It is not very effective when banks are steep and need a strong plant to hold them.

We think of Virginia creeper primarily in natural or naturalized settings, but it does have other uses. As a cover for stone walls and fences of wood or chain-link wire, this plant effectively softens hard architectural lines and lends a more natural look, and it can add density to fences that are not effective visual screens in themselves. Virginia creeper is not usually regarded as a high-climbing wallcover like its close relative, Boston ivy, but selections such as 'Saint Paulii,' with large numbers of adhesive tendril-tips, are fully as effective on brick walls as Boston ivy, and with greater cold-hardiness and power to naturalize architectural materials. Visitors to the world-famous Montreal Botanical Garden can see a magnificent example of high-climbing Virginia creeper covering one whole side of the Garden's massive administration building.

Further evidence of Virginia creeper's kinship to grapes is its susceptibility to grape diseases and insects. Fortunately, most of these usually are not serious. The most common disease is powdery mildew, which can disfigure the foliage in late summer and cause premature leaf-drop. This is most serious in sites having poor air circulation. While it seldom causes permanent damage, it can in some years eliminate bright autumn foliage. When necessary, it can be controlled by timely spraying.

Virginia creeper usually is not difficult to obtain in nurseries, but nonprofessionals with time and patience can propagate new plants by stem layering. This means burying a portion of stem in the soil in early summer, lightly notching the underside of the buried stem to induce formation of new roots at that point. A year later, when new roots have developed, the notched stem can be cut free from the parent plant and transplanted.

Once planted (pot-grown plants are easiest to transplant), the first year's growth may be disappointing, but a year or two later, well-established plants should be growing rapidly. From then on, this vine will earn its reputation as a functional, durable, and handsome landscape plant.

GROUND COVER PLANTS
(to 1½ feet tall)

II

GROUND COVERS ARE LOW PLANTS used in large numbers to provide a solid mass. By far the most common ground cover plants used in landscaping are turfgrasses. Our emphasis here is on other ground cover plants, useful where small spaces or steep slopes make it impractical to maintain turf, where growing conditions are not favorable for turf, or where other plants are simply needed for variety and seasonal beauty.

Ground covers range from inhabitants of shaded woodland floors, such as wild ginger (*Asarum canadense*), foamflower (*Tiarella cordifolia*), sweet woodruff (*Galium odoratum*), and mayapple (*Podophyllum peltatum*), to plants that grow in full sun on mountains and dunes, and even natives of swamps and bogs. Whole books have been written about ground cover plants, and scores of them are in use. Among them are plants adaptable to almost every conceivable climate and landscape site. Those that follow are well-adapted to cold climates, but can be supplemented by those listed above and many others, including bearberry (*Arctostaphylos uva-ursi*), low-growing cinquefoil (*Potentilla* species), lily-of-the-valley (*Convallaria majalis*), lowbush blueberry (*Vaccinium angustifolium*), moss pink (*Phlox subulata*), stonecrop (*Sedum* species), strawberries, and violets.

The Creeping Junipers

NOTHING WORKS BETTER THAN a low-growing juniper when a ground cover is needed for a dry, sunny spot. Junipers grow well in dry soils and are perhaps most useful on slopes where runoff keeps the ground particularly parched. When winter comes, their beauty continues, and some varieties undergo interesting color changes.

The largest number of cultivars, or horticultural varieties, of low-growing junipers are selections of creeping juniper (*Juniperus horizontalis*), a native of North America that grows wild as far east as the Atlantic coast of Nova Scotia and as far west as Alberta and Montana.

Selections of *J. horizontalis* are invariably low-growing, but some have ascending branches, reaching 18 to 20 inches above the ground, while others remain less than 4 inches tall. Most have the potential to spread to great width. I have seen single wild plants on the coast of Maine forming mats at least 40 feet across. But, with careful pruning when necessary, creeping junipers can function well in much more restricted situations.

Many selections of *J. horizontalis* have been made. The cultivars listed below are only a few of the possibilities, but they are generally available, and all are cold-hardy to −40°F.

'Bar Harbor,' a creeping form that originated in Maine, never grows more than 8 inches tall. Its foliage is a bluish green, taking on a silvery purplish cast in winter. Unfortunately, the name has been used for other creeping junipers native to coastal Maine, resulting in lack of uniformity among plants and confusion among growers.

'Douglasii' (Waukegan juniper) is not greatly different from 'Bar Harbor' but takes on a more metallic, purplish blue-green color in winter. It originated as a wild plant on the shores of Lake Michigan.

'Plumosa' (Andorra juniper) forms a dense ground cover with

26

branches ascending 12 to 18 inches. It turns plum-purple in winter.

'Wiltonii' (Blue Rug juniper) is a low, silvery blue-green selection. It forms a mat that, even after many years, reaches a height of only 4 inches or slightly higher at the center of the plant.

A few mat-forming cultivars can be found in a mountain variety of the common juniper (*Juniperus communis* var. *jackii*) from the Pacific Northwest. This variety has long, trailing branches that lie flat on the ground. Its deep blue-green foliage holds its color much better in winter than lowland forms of common juniper. The selection 'Gold Beach' has brighter green foliage, of equally elegant texture. Var. *jackii* and 'Gold Beach' have not been widely enough used for their adaptability to be fully known. They will certainly tolerate subzero temperatures and may be as cold-hardy as wild *J. communis*, which can stand temperatures of −40°F or lower in northeastern North America. Until their hardiness is better known, they should be planted cautiously in very cold areas.

Savin juniper (*J. sabina*), native to Europe and adjacent Asia, usually grows as a spreading-to-upright, vase-shaped plant, but at least two selections hold their branches close to the ground. 'Tamariscifolia' (Tamarix juniper), is a popular, handsome plant with feathery, rich green foliage. It reaches a height of 2 feet only after ten years or so. 'Broadmoor,' which is less common, remains below 1 foot in height for years and has brighter green foliage. Both selections are cold-hardy to at least −30°F.

Chinese juniper (*J. chinensis*) usually grows as a tree in the wild in Asia, but it is highly variable. The variety *sargentii* (Sargent juniper), which is native to northern Japan, stays less than 2 feet in height and makes an excellent ground cover in areas where temperatures do not fall below −30°F. Two selections, 'Glauca' and 'Viridis,' have blue-green and bright green foliage, respectively. The Japanese garden juniper (*J. chinensis* var. *procumbens*, sometimes considered a separate species and classified *J. procumbens*) apparently is extinct in its natural habitat, but it has been preserved in cultivation in Asia for centuries. It is similar to Sargent juniper in size and growth rate, but has needlelike, bristly foliage. A slower growing form of Japanese garden juniper, 'Nana,' stays below 1 foot for years, making an elegant, small-scale ground cover.

Low-growing junipers require little maintenance. When pruning is necessary to control size, it is best done by lifting branches and cutting them individually from underneath to retain the natural growth habit. They should never be sheared. Juniper blight can be a problem in some areas in moist growing seasons, but it usually is not serious enough in established landscapes to require control measures.

On balance, the low-growing junipers are hardy, drought-tolerant evergreens that function as effective year-round ground covers.

27

Mountain Ground Covers

ONE OF THE BENEFITS of mountain hiking is the fascinating display of mountain vegetation. Many hikers have wondered whether the mat-forming plants of alpine meadows can be cultivated as ground cover plants at lower elevations. The answer is that while some have peculiar requirements that are difficult to meet at lower elevations, others can be, and are being, used in man-made landscapes.

Before turning to specific examples, a general word of warning is in order. Mountain ecosystems are fragile and alpine plants already are suffering from an excess of hikers' boots. It is usually wrong and wasteful to contemplate collecting plants at high elevations for transplanting in gardens below. Not only does this contribute to depletion and ultimate extinction of these plants, but such efforts usually fail. It is possible to obtain plants of the examples mentioned here from nurseries that have grown them from seed, and establishing nursery-grown plants is not difficult.

Probably the most often planted mountain ground cover is the common lowbush blueberry (*Vaccinium angustifolium*). This plant not only supplies delicious edible blueberries in late summer, but it makes an excellent ground cover, remaining less than a foot tall, with bright green leaves that turn brilliant scarlet before falling in midautumn. The variety *laevifolium*, from the southern part of the range Newfoundland to Wisconsin and southward to the mountains of Virginia, is most widely available and best for fruit production. In good soil it may exceed a foot in height, but can be cut back to a lower height, if desired, in spring or early summer.

A more elegant evergreen relative of lowbush blueberry is the mountain cranberry (*Vaccinium vitis-idaea* var. *minus*). This slow-growing, creeping plant has lustrous convex leaves, only a quarter to a half inch long, that give outstanding textural interest. The foliage is so handsome that flowering and fruiting interest seem unnecessary. Nevertheless, the clusters of small clear pink, bell-shaped flowers add significantly to the charm of the plant in late spring or early summer, and the fruits, small cranberries less than a half inch across, provide considerable color in late summer and early autumn. Because of its elegant texture and slow growth, this plant is best used in small-scale gardens, where it can be appreciated at close range.

A relative of the blueberries and cranberries in the Heath family (Ericaceae) is Labrador tea (*Ledum groenlandicum*). This evergreen shrub with rusty, hairy foliage usually grows less than a foot tall in mountain habitats but can exceed this somewhat in cultivation. It resembles a tiny, hairy rhododendron, with leaves 1 to 2 inches long. In late spring or early summer it sends out white flowers in tight, globose clusters an inch or more across.

Wineleaf cinquefoil (*Potentilla tridentata*), a handsome evergreen ground cover native to mountains and bogs from Greenland to Georgia and Wisconsin, has lustrous, leathery, three-leaflet leaves. Leaflets are dark green, about half an inch long and toothed at the apex, giving the foliage mass fine texture and distinctive color, especially in autumn when the leaves turn wine red. The small white flowers, borne in loose clusters elevated well above the foliage mass, provide added interest in spring.

All four of these ground covers require acidic soil. This would be expected of the first three—all members of the Heath family—but it is also true for wineleaf cinquefoil, a member of the rose family. All four need well-drained, preferably sandy soil, and all are reasonably tolerant of drought, although less so in lowland areas with hot summers than in the coolness of their mountain habitats. Finally, all four are at their best when grown in full sun or light shade. Lowbush blueberry is tolerant of deep shade as well.

When growth requirements are satisfied these ground cover plants are relatively trouble free. They are at their best in the cool summers of their native habitat, or in cool coastal climates, but are more tolerant of heat than some other alpine plants. Nevertheless, they may fail to perform well at low elevations south of New York City because of the relatively long, hot summers.

All four of these plants are commercially available, but they will not be found in every nursery. In some areas it may be necessary to obtain them from distant specialists in alpine or ground cover plants. Any inconvenience encountered will be compensated for by these plants once they are established.

DECIDUOUS DWARF SHRUBS (1½ to 3 feet tall) III

SHRUBS IN THIS CATEGORY can be used for doorway accent, massing as a tall ground cover, or to add seasonal interest to rock gardens and other small-scale situations. They can also be planted at the front of a mixed shrub border, to cover lower branches of taller shrubs and add variety.

The modern trend toward smaller scale landscapes has made dwarf shrubs more popular and useful than they were years ago. The two old standbys described here are featured because of their cold-hardiness and bright yellow flowers in summer. Consider others as well, including daphne, daylilies, dyer's greenweed (*Genista tinctoria*), dwarf pea-shrubs (*Caragana* species), plantain-lilies (*Hosta* species), and low-growing roses and spireas.

31

Shrubby Cinquefoil

SHRUBBY CINQUEFOIL (*Potentilla fruticosa*) combines three important landscape assets. It remains low, in scale with small gardens and buildings; it flowers all summer long; and it is unusually tolerant of cold and drought.

This native of northern North America and northern Eurasia grows wild in areas having annual minimum temperatures as low as −40°F. Not all cultivars have been tried at temperatures this low, but most are hardy in the coldest areas of the northeastern United States and adjacent Canada.

Tolerance of salt spray makes shrubby cinquefoil a good choice for seaside planting and one of the best prospects to survive near salted walks and roadways. As happens with many other plants, salt-tolerance is accompanied by drought-tolerance, and this shrub is very much at home in dry, sunny spots.

Flowers of shrubby cinquefoil, about an inch across, are bright yellow in most plants but pale yellow or white in a few cultivars. They begin to open in early summer and sometimes continue until first frost. Some cultivars flower more heavily and more continuously than others, but all are showy through most of the summer. Bright green, finely cut foliage supplements flowering interest, then falls without much color change in midautumn. Young leaves of some cultivars are covered with silky hairs, giving the new growth a slightly silvered look.

Since seasonal interest is limited to summer and early autumn at best, this shrub is a natural for planting at summer cottages and in areas where snow comes early and stays late. It is an ideal plant for dooryard accent or the front of a shrub border. Since it can be counted on to remain below 3 feet in height (some cultivars grow only half that tall), it is also useful for foundation planting, even below windows.

Shrubby cinquefoil does have a few limitations. In some areas it has become a weed by invading marginal pastures where growth of forage plants is weak. Even though this may breed contempt for the plant among residents of such areas, the weed problem is not usually a serious one.

Chewing insects such as Japanese beetle and rose chafer can temporarily disfigure both flowers and foliage. Before selecting this plant, it might save trouble later to determine whether other plants in the neighborhood have often experienced such damage. Powdery mildew also can mar the foliage in some areas. Where this is a problem, it is a good idea to plant in breezy spots, as good air circulation alone sometimes will control mildew.

In those rare instances where insect or disease problems are so great as to require spraying, it may be simpler to substitute other plants, such as the St. Johnswort (*Hypericum* species), than to provide a higher level of maintenance. In other ways, shrubby cinquefoil is easy to care for. Pruning is seldom if ever necessary, but if old plants should become straggly they can be reshaped by drastic renewal pruning—cutting down to stubs in early spring.

A number of good cultivars are on the market, and choice will be limited by availability at any time and place. For bright golden yellow flowers, none is more colorful than 'Goldfinger,' a relatively recent arrival on the horticultural scene. Its flowers are an inch or more across and borne in great numbers. Other cultivars with golden yellow flowers include 'Gold Drop' (also called 'Farreri'), 'Klondike,' and 'Sutter's Gold.' Cultivars with lighter, lemon yellow flowers include 'Katherine Dykes,' 'Lemon Drop,' and 'Longacre.' 'Tangerine' has slightly deeper yellow flowers, while those of 'Moonlight' (also called 'Manelys') and 'Primrose Beauty' are delicately pale yellow.

A few selections have been made for white flowers (with yellow stamens in the center). Probably the finest of these is 'Abbotswood,' with large white flowers, deep blue-green foliage, and compact form. 'Mount Everest' is a less desirable alternative.

Recently there has been great interest in red-flowering cinquefoils. 'Red Ace,' a fairly recent selection, is very low growing and may not be as cold-hardy as other cultivars, but needs further trial. Its flowers are reddish orange at best and merely orange in some climates.

New orange or red-flowering cultivars probably will continue to appear, and at some point a red cultivar with good foliage and form may be developed. Meanwhile, thoroughly tested cultivars of shrubby cinquefoil offer a range of color from white through several shades to deep yellow. These plants are excellent sources of summer color and functional low shrubs in the bargain.

St. Johnsworts

LOW-GROWING SHRUBS ARE ALWAYS AT A PREMIUM, especially those with broad seasonal interest. The St. Johnsworts (*Hypericum* species) are neat and compact, require little or no pruning, and offer striking summer flowers without becoming unattractive in other seasons. In spite of these advantages they are, strangely, not widely used.

St. Johnsworts grow wild throughout much of the temperate and subtropical zones of the Northern Hemisphere. Even though there are some 200 known species, few are useful where winter temperatures regularly fall below 0°F. But those few can play an important role in home landscapes.

The hardy St. Johnsworts share several traits. They all have sparkling golden yellow flowers in midsummer, lasting from two to four weeks, followed by yellow-green, beaked seed capsules. Their neatly textured, smooth-margined, bright to bluish green leaves contrast in color and texture with other shrubs and remain green well into autumn. Last, and perhaps most important, they remain low, from knee- to waist-high, without pruning.

St. Johnsworts grow and flower best in full sun, but also perform reasonably well in partial shade. Tolerant of differing soil conditions, they thrive on dry, sandy soils, as well as those that are moderately moist, and they are adapted to a wide range of soil acidity.

Maintenance requirements are modest. Pruning is unnecessary except to rejuvenate old or damaged plants. Several diseases are known, but are seldom serious enough to require corrective action. All things considered, St. Johnsworts enhance the landscape while requiring notably little upkeep in return.

The hardiest of the group is the Kalm St. Johnswort (*Hypericum kalmianum*), named for the eighteenth-century Swedish naturalist,

Peter Kalm. This species is native from Quebec to Illinois and usefully hardy in areas where annual minimum temperatures average as low as −30°F, which includes most of New England, New York, all of the Great Lakes area, and the southern half of Minnesota and Wisconsin. This shrub remains below 3 feet in height and at the approach of midsummer bears large numbers of bright yellow flowers, each up to an inch wide, mostly in clusters of three. Foliage of Kalm St. Johnswort is unusually fine-textured, the individual leaves 1 to 2 inches long, but only about a quarter inch wide, and bluish green. The looseness of the foliage exposes the stems, with their smooth, seemingly polished, brown bark. This plant is best used in a mixed shrub border, for its color and textural contrast, or as a specimen for accent in small-scale situations where paving and architectural details dominate over plant material.

Shrubby St. Johnswort (*Hypericum prolificum*) is a more vigorous shrub, sometimes reaching a height of 4 feet, with leaves 2 to 3 inches long and a half inch wide. Its flowering is similar to that of Kalm St. Johnswort but slightly later, and it makes an excellent rounded specimen for the shrub border or foundation planting. It is slightly less cold-hardy than *Hypericum kalmianum*, being fully reliable only in areas where annual minimum temperatures normally do not fall below −20°F.

Other shrubby St. Johnsworts are available for milder areas, but most are reliable only where the temperature remains above −15°F. Among the most common of these are golden St. Johnswort (*H. frondosum*) and its low-growing cultivar 'Sunburst,' and the goldencup St. Johnswort (*H. patulum*) and its cultivars 'Henryi,' 'Hidcote,' and 'Sungold.'

In addition to the shrubby forms of St. Johnswort, there are a few trailing species. The Blue Ridge St. Johnswort (*H. buckleyi*), as the name suggests, is native to the southern Appalachian Mountains. Its creeping form, with occasional stems rising to a foot or so before falling of their own weight, makes it an effective ground cover, but fully reliable only where temperatures seldom drop below −10°F. Aaronsbeard St. Johnswort (*Hypericum calycinum*) is more tender, but makes a superb, vigorous ground cover in areas to which it is adapted. Its flowers, golden yellow and 2 to 3 inches across, displayed against the solid mass of dark green foliage, make it one of the most ornamental of the St. Johnsworts and one of the most handsome of all ground covers.

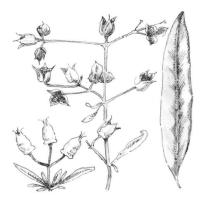

It would seem futile to attempt to use these trailing species in the North Country, and they certainly cannot be recommended there. But it is a great temptation to experiment with them in areas having reliable snow cover for winter protection. On the other hand, there are shrubby forms for nearly any climate in the northeastern United States. Careful selection will yield striking summer color and a plant that is presentable in all seasons and requires little effort from the gardener.

35

DECIDUOUS LOW SHRUBS
(3 to 6 feet tall)

IV

SHRUBS IN THIS GROUP ARE USEFUL for mass-planting without fully obstructing vision, for corner planting around one-story buildings, or for seasonal variety in mixed shrub borders. They have gained in popularity with recent trends toward smaller homes and gardens.

The low shrubs that follow offer wide variety in seasonal interest and adaptability, but they are by no means a complete list of possibilities. Others to consider include Japanese barberry (*Berberis thunbergii*), sweetshrub (*Calycanthus floridus*), leatherwood (*Dirca palustris*), kerria, the true Persian lilac (*Syringa* x *persica*), low azaleas, dwarf shrub honeysuckles, the lower-growing serviceberries (*Amelanchier florida* and *A. stolonifera*), and certain roses and spireas in this height range.

Bayberry

WHEN THE FIRST EUROPEAN SETTLERS reached the shores of eastern North America, they probably were impressed by thickets of an unusual plant with pleasantly aromatic leaves and gray, waxy berries— a shrub that we call bayberry (*Myrica pensylvanica*). They would have had this pleasure landing on almost any part of the Atlantic coastline, for this plant and its close relative wax myrtle (*M. cerifera*) together make up a range that extends from Newfoundland to Florida, and to Texas as well.

Wax myrtle, native and widely used in the southeastern states, is a handsome shrub, similar in general appearance to bayberry but larger and considerably less cold-hardy—too tender to be a serious prospect for use in the Northeast. Sweet gale (*Myrica gale*), an inhabitant of far northern swamps, is a potential landscape plant for climates too cold for bayberry, but it is almost never used and probably not commercially available.

In addition to its obvious landscape interest, bayberry is unusually site-tolerant, highly functional, and essentially trouble free. When we realize that this shrub has been included in North American landscape plantings for well over 250 years, it is surprising that it is not more widely used today.

The coastal habitat of bayberry suggests that it would be salt-tolerant enough to be useful near salted walks in northern areas. This does seem to be true. It is also tolerant of dry, infertile soils. In fact, it remains in excellent condition in the poorest soils, presumably because of its ability to utilize atmospheric nitrogen with the help of microorganisms living in association with its roots.

Under ideal conditions, bayberry may reach heights up to 10 feet. But usually it is safer not to expect it to become that large, especially in northern climates. In northern areas, it may suffer some top-kill in severe winters, remaining well below eye level. Where it is fully hardy, growing in full sun and reasonably moist but well-drained soil, it will function as an effective visual screen, although it may need light pruning to encourage fullness. Used as a low massing plant, its height can be controlled easily by pruning if necessary, and it is useful in areas where annual minimum temperatures average −25°F to −30°F.

The foliage of bayberry, varying in shade from bright to deep green, is slightly leathery and persists late into autumn. It is strongly and pleasantly aromatic when crushed. Other parts of the plant are also aromatic, including the wax that covers the fruits. Early settlers used bayberry wax to add scent to hand-made candles, and modern candlemakers still do.

Even though the fruit is of less interest visually than foliage during the growing season, the berries persist after leaf-drop, adding interest in winter. Bayberry is dioecious—that is, individual plants are either male or female—so not all plants will bear fruit, but the non-fruiting, male plants are necessary to pollinate the flowers of nearby female plants. To ensure pollination when fruiting interest is desired, landscapers will commonly arrange mass plantings of bayberry.

In addition to its other good qualities, bayberry is usually troublefree. It can be affected by leaf spot diseases and virus, but they are seldom serious problems. One potential maintenance problem is bayberry's tendency to grow root suckers, and that should be considered in deciding where to plant it. When it is used as a mass planting surrounded by pavement, suckering is not a problem, but rather helps to keep the plant mass full and resistant to weed encroachment.

Since bayberry grows wild over such a broad geographic range, and presumably varies widely in response to climate, it is a good idea to use plants grown from native material as close as possible geographically to the landscape site. At the least, it is risky to use material from the southern Atlantic Coast in New England or the Midwest, or material from the Canadian Maritime Provinces or New England in the southern states.

Even though bayberry grows wild in the more-or-less maritime climates of the Atlantic Coast, it seems to be well adapted to the continental climates of the Midwest. It appears that this long underused plant has great potential as a trouble-free, functional, and attractive landscape plant for all but the very coldest climates of the northeastern United States.

Bridalwreath Spirea

AS A CHILD GROWING UP IN CENTRAL VERMONT I became familiar with a graceful shrub that we called bridalwreath. Later I found that in other places the same plant is more often called Vanhoutte spirea, while the name bridalwreath is reserved for another species of spirea. And so I became aware of the confusion that can be caused by regional vernacular names, and I learned the value of knowing plants by their botanical names.

More than fifty natural species of spirea are listed in Alfred Rehder's *Manual of Cultivated Trees and Shrubs*. Less than half belong to the same group as the bridalwreath spireas, and only a half-dozen are at all common in cold climates.

My childhood bridalwreath—Vanhoutte spirea (*Spiraea* x *vanhouttei*), to avoid confusion—grows to about 5 or 6 feet in height, with multitudes of single flowers in rounded clusters arranged along the graceful branches. By the time it flowers, in late spring, the foliage has also appeared, and it serves as a striking background for the white flowers. The leaves are dull blue-green and roughly fan-shaped. Usually they do not change color much in autumn, but in certain cold spots, in some years, they go through a brief but beautiful orange-pink phase before falling. This hybrid shrub has been in use in eastern North America for more than a century. It dots the landscape of virtually every town and village in the Northeast, even in areas where winter temperatures fall to − 30°F.

Threelobe spirea (*Spiraea trilobata*), a native of northern Asia, is somewhat smaller than Vanhoutte spirea, seldom growing taller than 4 or 5 feet. It is not quite as showy, either, but it makes a graceful display of white flowers at about the same time as Vanhoutte spirea. Its most important feature is that it is cold-hardy in the most severe climates of the United States, in areas where annual minimum temperatures average −35°F to −40°F. Although threelobe spirea is not widely available, it is worth seeking out for very cold climates.

The plant most widely called bridalwreath, *Spiraea prunifolia*, is a shrub 6 to 8 feet tall at maturity, with gracefully arching branches bearing large numbers of double, buttonlike flowers in midspring. It is unusual among spireas because of its glossy leaves, which turn clear orange-red in autumn. This is one of the finest of all spireas, but it is cold-hardy only in areas where annual minimum temperatures do not usually fall below −20°F.

Another exceedingly graceful shrub is the garland spirea (*Spiraea* x *arguta*), a complex hybrid involving at least three Eurasian species. The small leaves of this shrub give it fine texture, and its tiny flowers, appearing in large numbers before the leaves have fully expanded in spring, lend a graceful, billowy appearance at that season. This shrub is variable in both size and cold-hardiness. The compact, low-growing selection 'Compacta' remains below eye level for a long time if planted in full sun and is hardier than average for the species, functioning well in areas where annual minimum temperatures average −25°F.

Thunberg spirea (*Spiraea thunbergii*), one of the parents of garland spirea, is similar in effect but has brighter green, fine-textured foliage that turns a delicate golden orange in autumn. Unfortunately, it is less cold-hardy than garland spirea, but is useful in areas where annual minimum temperatures average no lower than −15°F to −20°F.

Some generalizations can be made about spireas. First, they perform best in full sun and well-drained soil, although most tolerate some shade and occasional wetness. Second, they are relatively trouble free, but most require pruning by thinning out main branches every few years to keep them in good form. Third, they have slender stems and rather fine texture.

Many spireas do not become tall enough for use as a visual screen, and few of those that do are dense enough to carry out that function very well. On the other hand, many are effective in an informal hedge or mass planted to separate areas without blocking views. And most, especially the bridalwreath types, are graceful in form, especially when their branches are accentuated by the flowers.

Spireas have a nostalgic charm for many people, and they blend especially well into restorations of nineteenth-century landscapes. Several, especially those that remain below eye level, work equally well in modern-day residential landscapes. Although they are not as versatile as viburnums, they are serviceable, strikingly graceful, and beautiful when in flower.

Fragrant Sumac

THE SUMAC GENUS, *Rhus*, well known for its poisonous members, also includes several non-poisonous species that serve as functional and colorful landscape plants. One of the most useful is fragrant sumac (*Rhus aromatica*), a thicket-forming native shrub that provides exceptional autumnal color.

Growing wild from New England to Minnesota and as far south as Florida and Louisiana, fragrant sumac is valued as a landscape plant in much of the eastern United States and adjacent Canada. As a wild shrub it grows in full sun and dry, gravelly soil, where few other woody plants offer competition. But it is useful in landscaping since it adapts to different conditions, from full sun to considerable shade and to almost any well-drained soil. It will tolerate seashore conditions and small amounts of de-icing salts near walks and roadways in the snow belt.

In addition to tolerating a variety of sites, fragrant sumac adapts well to the climate of the northeastern and central states, including areas where average annual minimum temperatures reach −35°F, with occasional plunges even lower.

This shrub offers seasonal interest from early spring through autumn. Its small, pale yellow flowers are not showy, but since they emerge in early spring before the leaves and when there is little other color in the landscape, their contribution is significant. The leaves, which are aromatic when crushed, are made up of three leaflets covered with soft hairs. Sumac leaves only vaguely resemble poison ivy's usually larger, smooth leaves. As the foliage turns deeper green in midsummer, small clusters of fuzzy red fruits develop on plants grown in full sun. But the real show comes in autumn, when the foliage turns yellow, overlaid with brilliant red-orange. This change may not be so spectacular in heavy soils, but plants in relatively dry soils, growing in full sun, almost always provide autumn color.

Fragrant sumac typically tends to trail along the ground with ascending branches growing rather quickly to about 3 feet tall, and to twice that height in some forms. Even the low forms, once fully established, are tall enough to function as barriers to pedestrian traffic. Because it tolerates dry soil, fragrant sumac is especially useful for covering banks where much of the rainfall runs off rather than soaking in. Its size and rapid growth rule it out as a small-scale ground cover, but for roadside planting and other large expanses it is very effective.

Landscape requirements often dictate selection of the low-growing forms (to 3 feet tall) in preference to the tall forms (6 feet). Wild plants in the eastern United States usually are low-growing and can be transplanted directly or used as parents for propagation with some assurance that they will remain low. But in the Midwest, many wild plants are of the tall type, and when low plants are needed it is safer to use material that has been selected and propagated for low, spreading growth. 'Gro-Low' is one of these selections.

Plant shape can be modified by pruning, of course, but it is simpler to start with an appropriate form. When shrubs are selected to fit the size requirements of the planting site, pruning may be needed to trim back an occasional unruly branch, but not to combat the natural growth tendency. Old plantings that have become ragged can be renewed by cutting the entire tops down to stubs about 6 inches from the ground. This trimming should be done in spring or early summer, so that the stubble will soon be covered with lush and tidy new growth, and to allow as much time as possible for new growth before autumn. Occasional pruning of leading branch tips promotes greater fullness.

One of fragrant sumac's most practical features is that it is seldom bothered by insects and diseases and so requires little or no maintenance other than weeding during establishment, and occasional pruning thereafter. This resistance is an obvious asset in any landscape plant, especially in one so likely to be used on a large scale.

Like many other native plants, fragrant sumac is not available in every nursery. But neither is it rare. A little extra effort in obtaining this plant will be amply repaid by its functional effectiveness, adaptability, ease of care, and seasonal interest.

Korean Abelialeaf

IN MUCH OF THE EASTERN UNITED STATES, forsythia is the anticipated herald of impending spring. But fully as interesting is a close relative, Korean abelialeaf, which has white flowers on leafless, wand-like stems in April. And abelialeaf may be more widely adapted to cold climates than forsythia.

Korean abelialeaf (*Abeliophyllum distichum*) so much resembles a white forsythia that it is sometimes called that in garden catalogs. It is lower-growing than all but one or two dwarf varieties of forsythia, rarely exceeding 5 feet in height, often only waist-high. Its flowers open before there are leaves to obscure or dilute their color, and are particularly effective when displayed against a dark background of evergreens or the shady side of a building. The flowers are smaller than those of most varieties of forsythia, and sometimes take on a pink tinge if they open slowly during a period of very cool weather. Like other early spring flowers, they run considerable risk of damage from late spring freezes. In inland areas, with fluctuating spring temperatures, the floral display of abelialeaf comes a bit earlier than forsythia bloom, and sometimes ends abruptly if the thermometer drops to 20°F or so. This risk is no less farther south, since flowers open earlier there and are prone to correspondingly earlier spring freezes. Closer to the sea or near inland bodies of water, which have a stabilizing influence on temperature, flowering is sometimes delayed by the slow arrival of spring. With less risk of severe freezing, full flowering is more reliable in these locations. Even so, I know of a fifteen-year-old planting of Korean abelialeaf in northern Vermont; far from maritime influences, it is nevertheless fairly reliable in bloom.

In addition to late spring freezes, extreme winter cold poses a further problem. Abelialeaf, like forsythia and many other spring-flowering shrubs, initiates flower buds during the summer before bloom. These almost microscopic primordial flowers must survive winter in dormant buds in order to develop into flowers in spring. Most forsythia flower buds will withstand temperatures of −15°F to −20°F when fully dormant in midwinter. Those of Korean abelialeaf will sometimes withstand −20°F to −25°F under similar conditions. Northern winters with occasional cold snaps to −25°F or lower will kill dormant flower buds that are not protected by deep snow, so there is a northern limit for full flowering in any particular year. The colder the climate, the less chance of significant spring flowering, and in the far northern parts of the Northeast there is little point in using these plants except in extremely sheltered sites or "microclimates." For what it is worth, stems of both abelialeaf and forsythia are far hardier than their flower buds. But without flowering interest, these plants attract few admirers.

The summer foliage of Korean abelialeaf is dark green and lustrous, varying in length from 2 to 3 inches low on vigorous shoots, to less than 1 inch on stem tips bearing the next spring's flower buds. The leaves are oval, pointed, and untoothed, and apparently reminded the Japanese botanist who named this plant of the leaves of abelia—a fine, broadleafed evergreen plant useful only in milder climates. In autumn, the leaves develop a purple overcast and remain that color until they fall.

Korean abelialeaf has no peculiar site requirements, but will perform best if located away from strong winds, in reasonably fertile soil. For best flowering in spring, plants should be exposed to sun for at least half the day in summer. A combination of morning sun and afternoon shade will accomplish this; shade late in the day will help to delay flowering in spring and so reduce the risk of flowers' freezing after they open. This plant grows well on virtually all well-drained soils in the Northeast, but like most garden and landscape plants, it will benefit from additions of organic matter to the soil. Once established, it will add a graceful touch of white to the early spring landscape, a spot of lustrous dark green in summer, and a deep purplish green later, to contrast with autumn's more vivid colors.

45

Korean Spice Viburnum

LANDSCAPE PERCEPTIONS ARE PRIMARILY VISUAL for most people, but plants can add delight through the other senses as well. If we were to rate landscape plants according to how many of the senses they stimulate, Korean spice viburnum (*Viburnum carlesii*) would be at least a three-star selection, appealing to sight, smell, and touch.

The visual features of this shrub alone are enough to justify its use. In early spring, its flower buds, borne in clusters 2 to 3 inches across, swell and turn rosy pink. The flowers open pink at first, then white at full bloom. After flowering, the soft green leaves make a dense mass that provides background for the ripening berries as they turn from green to bright red and finally to black in autumn. Foliage usually turns dull red in autumn, to round out a full growing season.

The delightful clovelike fragrance of its flowers gives this shrub its name. Flowers of other plants are as delicious or as pervasive in their fragrance, but few combine delicacy with power of fragrance in quite the same way.

When the leaves of Korean spice viburnum first expand, they are soft and velvety to the touch, but later in the summer they take on a more sandpapery texture. At either time, one who has felt the leaves of this shrub would probably recognize them while blindfolded.

Even though the esthetic qualities of Korean spice viburnum are sufficient to recommend it, this shrub is functional as well. Not reliably tall enough at 5 to 6 feet to serve as a visual screen, it is still useful for massing and foundation planting in spots where it will not block low windows. The excellent low-growing selection 'Compactum' remains below 4 feet in height for years and can be used where the species type would be a bit too tall.

This Korean native is hardy in all but the very coldest zones of the Northeast and as far north as southern Minnesota in the Midwest. It grows well in any soil that is well-drained but not drought-prone, and tolerates partial shade but flowers and fruits best in full sun.

Korean spice viburnum has very few problems, but one of them can be serious. In the past, difficulties in seedling and cutting propagation have led nurseries to graft this plant on rootstocks of another viburnum, wayfaring tree (*Viburnum lantana*). A disease of the graft union can be troublesome, but even when disease is not present, the more vigorous wayfaring tree understock may overgrow and overwhelm the grafted scion, sending up additional shoots from below the graft union. When not detected and removed, these shoots overgrow the Korean spice viburnum within a few years. This gives rise to claims that one kind of plant has mysteriously changed into another kind, a phenomenon also frequently reported by uninitiated growers of garden roses. The lesson in the story is that there is nothing mysterious in such happenings; they are simply the result of a grafted variety being crowded out by an overly exuberant understock. Thanks to advances in propagation methods, nurseries are now rooting cuttings of Korean spice viburnum, and the resulting "own-rooted" plants are more trouble free than grafted plants, which still show up occasionally.

Korean spice viburnum has been hybridized with several related viburnums. Some of the resulting hybrids are useful landscape plants in their own right. Three of the best are Burkwood viburnum, fragrant snowball, and Judd viburnum.

Burkwood viburnum (V. x *burkwoodii*), a hybrid by a tender evergreen viburnum, has small, lustrous, deep green leaves that remain on the plant until early winter. Considering its parentage, this plant is surprisingly winter-hardy, withstanding average minimum temperatures of −15°F and occasional drops to −25°F. It is tall enough for visual screening at 8 to 10 feet, but too loose in growth habit to be fully effective. Its flowers are similar to those of Korean spice viburnum in appearance and fragrance, but it is the lustrous, fine-textured, semi-evergreen foliage that gives this plant its distinctive landscape value.

Fragrant snowball (V. x *carlcephalum*), a hybrid of another rather tender viburnum, is similar to the Korean spice viburnum parent in hardiness but differs in its greater stature (to 8 feet) and suitability for screening, and in its larger flower clusters. Judd viburnum (V. x *juddii*) is a hybrid of Korean spice viburnum by another hardy species. It is as adaptable as Korean spice viburnum, easier to propagate by cuttings, and somewhat taller and looser in habit. Even though it is an excellent landscape plant, it is not so widely available as the other viburnums mentioned.

Whether Korean spice viburnum, its cultivar 'Compactum,' or a hybrid is used will depend on the size and function needed, and the foliar effect desired. In any case, the result will be spring flowers with superlative fragrance, and broad appeal to other senses during the entire leafy season.

Meyer Lilac

WHEN WE THINK OF LILACS, several impressions come to mind: fragrance of flowers, nostalgia, tradition—but plants too large for use around most modern-day dwellings. Meyer lilac, on the contrary, is a small, compact shrub with almost scentless flowers, so new to landscape use that it hardly can have traditional value, much less bring on nostalgia. Yet it is a lilac, and probably the most useful landscape plant of all lilacs.

Meyer lilac (*Syringa meyeri*) is sometimes offered for sale under the name of *Syringa palibiniana*, and is often called "dwarf Korean lilac," even though it is not from Korea but from northern China. This handsome small shrub flowers at the same time as the common lilac and its French hybrids, with deep purple buds opening into medium violet flowers that quickly fade to pale lavender. Flower clusters are smaller than those of most lilacs, but perfectly in scale with the size of the plant. Unfortunately, flowers are not fragrant, but this is more than compensated for by their appearance on very young plants, often no more than 2 feet tall. The plant's landscape interest is continued after flowering by its refined, lustrous foliage, usually free of the powdery mildew disease that disfigures many other lilacs in late summer.

The outstanding feature of Meyer lilac in the landscape is its compact growth. Seldom will plants exceed 5 feet in height and 6 feet in spread. In far northern climates and in poor soils they will remain under 4 feet without pruning for many years, perhaps indefinitely. Clearly this is not a plant for visual screening!

This versatile lilac can be planted against the foundation of a home without later obscuring the view from picture windows. It can be planted in front of tall, leggy shrubs as a "facing" shrub, to cover their bare lower branches. It can also be used to supplement the seasonal interest of other plants in a mixed border. Or it can be used as a specimen, to serve as a center of interest in an intimate garden, or to draw attention to an entrance. The ideal time for planting is as early as possible in the spring.

Meyer lilac is hardy in the coldest areas in the Northeast, to temperatures of −40°F and lower. It also has been fully successful for more than ten years in tests in the north-central states, including North Dakota and Minnesota, in a cooperative experimental project among state universities and the U.S. Department of Agriculture.

Adaptability of Meyer lilac to different soils is equally impressive. It grows well on both light and heavy soils. Once established, it tolerates the occasional dryness of sandy soils, remaining more dwarf than on richer soils. But it will still benefit from an occasional soaking during unusually dry periods. Soil that is occasionally wet should pose no problem for this plant, but it cannot be expected to perform well in soil that is chronically poorly drained. Much has been written about lilacs and soil acidity; the fact is that they grow well over a wide range of soil acidity. Variations that occur in the Northeast make very little difference to the growth of Meyer lilac, or lilacs in general.

Another important feature of this landscape plant is that it is seldom bothered by insects or diseases—certainly not enough to justify a preventive spray program—although an occasional infestation by scale insects may require timely attention. Maintenance in the form of pruning is equally unnecessary, thanks to the plant's neat, compact growth. It is not even necessary to remove dead flowers in order to promote flowering the following spring, as is true for many other lilacs.

To find Meyer lilac in nurseries or nursery catalogs, look for it under its correct name (*Syringa meyeri*), or the often-used but incorrect synonyms *Syringa palibiniana* or dwarf Korean lilac. When it is growing in your yard, you will be able to enjoy the company of one of the finest of all dwarf flowering shrubs, an aristocrat among lilacs, and one that is adaptable to the most difficult of northern climates.

49

Rugosa Rose

SHRUBS THAT NEVER GROW ABOVE EYE LEVEL are in great demand for residential landscapes. Those that remain interesting over a major part of the year are particularly desirable, and it goes without saying that any useful and attractive shrub that can tolerate our coldest winters will be well received. Rugosa rose (*Rosa rugosa*) meets all of those qualifications, which explains why it's so widely used in the North Country as a landscape plant and as a parent of garden hybrids.

Native to China, Japan, and Korea, rugosa rose is so well adapted to the northeastern United States and adjacent Canada that it has become naturalized in some areas. Fortunately, it has not spread so widely as to become a serious weed problem like that other Japanese species, the famous (or infamous) multiflora (*Rosa multiflora*), which is not hardy in northern areas, but is so aggressive and fast-growing where it is hardy that it cannot be considered a useful plant for residential landscaping. Certain forms of rugosa rose are cold-hardy in parts of Manitoba and Minnesota where average annual minimum temperatures fall below −35°F and where "cold" winters can bring temperatures as low as −50°F. No wonder northern residents appreciate this plant!

Not only is rugosa rose cold-hardy; its tolerance of salt spray is nearly legendary. Extensive plantings in highway medians in Rhode Island were thriving only a few hundred yards from Narragansett Bay in the 1960s, and presumably still are. Such salt-tolerance qualifies this shrub for planting near salted walks and roadways in colder inland climates, but it should be remembered that some roadside sites are so thoroughly salt-polluted that no woody plants can survive. Another advantage of rugosa rose is that it is a low-maintenance shrub in most northern areas. Even though no rose is entirely free of insect and disease problems, this species is troubled less by them than most.

Many of the hardy roses are mediocre landscape plants because of poor form and foliage, but rugosa rose is an exception. Its lustrous,

50

leathery foliage is highly rugose (textured with deeply impressed veins), making an interesting dark green mass in summer and frequently turning a beautiful golden orange before falling in autumn. The entire plant usually forms a regular mound, with foliage all the way to the ground once the shrub is well established. This form makes it useful as an individual specimen, in the shrub border, or for informal hedges and large-scale massing.

Pruning of rugosa rose is seldom necessary except to remove dead wood, but plants may be pruned to keep them below their natural height of 5 to 6 feet. Even when the full size is not objectionable, severe renewal pruning (cutting the entire top down to stubs) may be helpful for old plants that have become open and ungainly. Such pruning should be done in spring or early summer, to allow plenty of time for regrowth and acclimation before winter sets in.

Although flowering interest is not this plant's only claim to fame, it is considerable. The fragrant rose-purple, pink, or white flowers, up to 3 inches across, appear in early summer and, with adequate moisture, continue intermittently for several weeks. The wild type of rugosa rose has single flowers exposing large clusters of golden yellow stamens in the center, but some of the hybrids have double flowers.

The distinctive fruits of roses are called hips. Those of rugosa rose are very large, frequently a full inch or more across, and bright red-orange, providing significant landscape interest in late summer and early autumn. In moist seasons, early fruits and late flowers can be seen on plants at the same time in late summer. The edible hips, a rich source of ascorbic acid (vitamin C), are used for making teas and preserves.

In addition to the useful species type of rugosa rose, several selections and hybrids are also available. A few of the more common ones are listed here: 'Blanc Double de Coubert' has fragrant, pure white, semi-double flowers, outstanding foliage, and large orange-red fruits. 'F. J. Grootendorst' has double, rose-pink flowers that are only about one inch across but are borne in clusters and usually bloom all summer. 'Pink Grootendorst' is similar, but with pink flowers. 'Hansa,' very popular in the northern Central Plains, is exceptionally cold-hardy, with fragrant, double, purplish red flowers that bloom all summer. 'Max Graf' is a distinctive trailing hybrid with pink flowers, useful as a ground cover, but hardy in the extreme north only if there is a heavy winter snow cover. This list is not all-inclusive. Other cultivars can sometimes be obtained from nurseries specializing in old-fashioned or shrub-type roses.

Rugosa rose and its hybrids provide a long seasonal show of flowers, foliage, and fruits. They require minimum maintenance and offer maximum reliability in cold climates, and serve as highly functional landscape plants in a variety of situations.

DECIDUOUS MEDIUM SHRUBS
(6 to 12 feet tall)

V

SHRUBS IN THIS SIZE GROUP are tall enough at maturity to serve as visual screens. How effective they are depends on their density as well as their height. Visual screens are important in most landscapes. They provide separation between outdoor areas, give privacy, and block undesirable views. They are the walls between outdoor living areas.

A visual screen may be just an informal hedge of medium or large shrubs, planted close enough together to form a solid mass. Plants in such screens usually must be pruned carefully while they are young to encourage low branching and a well-filled-in base. When enough space is available, shrubs can be planted in a double, alternating row, making a still denser screen. For more informality and broader seasonal interest, use a mixed planting with enough medium and large shrubs to provide height and enough dwarf and low shrubs to fill in the base of the border and provide color in different seasons.

Good candidates for visual screens can be found among the medium shrubs that follow and the tall shrubs in the next section. Still other good possibilities will be found in retail nurseries.

53

Cranberry Bushes

WHEN EUROPEAN SETTLERS ARRIVED in the New England colonies, they brought with them a fast-growing shrub with red berries called European cranberry bush (*Viburnum opulus*). This import became established as a landscape plant in North America before many people noticed that a very similar plant was already growing wild in many of the areas being settled. We now know that the American cranberry bush (*Viburnum trilobum*) has all the landscape versatility and beauty of its European relative, and greater hardiness and fall foliage color as well.

American cranberry bush grows wild in many parts of northern New England, New York, and adjacent Canada eastward to Nova Scotia. Its range also extends westward through the Great Lakes region and all the way to Oregon. Much farther west, a third cranberry bush (*Viburnum sargentii*) grows wild in northeastern Asia. The three cranberry bushes are so similar that some botanists do not recognize them as separate species, but consider them all to be varieties of *Viburnum opulus*.

The cranberry bushes reach heights of 10–12 feet and eventually spread to at least 6–8 feet. Large plants remain full with little or no pruning, and are effective as visual screens during the leafy season. New leaf growth begins in midspring, and by late spring or early summer mature plants are covered with small, white flowers in flat clusters as much as 4 inches across, displayed against deep green, maplelike leaves. Fertile flowers toward the center of each cluster are inconspicuous, but are surrounded by an outer ring of more showy flowers, giving a "lace-doily" effect to the flat cluster. The outer flowers are sterile, but bright red berries develop from the small inner ones, providing color from late summer through autumn. They hold on, shriveled, to serve as winter food for hungry birds. The foliage of the European cranberry bush remains deep green until it falls in midautumn, but the leaves of the American cranberry bush usually turn dull red before dropping.

American cranberry bush fruits are sometimes harvested as "high-bush cranberries" and used for making sauce and preserves. When cooked, they release an odor reminiscent of that produced by an excited skunk. Fortunately, the odor does not remain to taint the cooked product, but it could dampen the cook's enthusiasm for repeating the effort another year.

Superior selections of American cranberry bush such as 'Andrews' and 'Wentworth' may be difficult to find in nurseries, but 'Compactum,' selected for compact growth, is more widely available. This variety is useful in smaller-scale landscape situations, since it remains more narrowly upright than the wild type and does not grow tall so quickly.

American cranberry bush, like other cranberry bushes, thrives in full sun or light shade, in any reasonably fertile, well-drained soil. It is adaptable, as its native range suggests, to just about any part of the northern United States and adjacent Canada—even to areas that experience temperatures as low as −35°F to −40°F.

Among the related cranberry bushes, there are a few noteworthy cultivars. The so-called European snowball (*Viburnum opulus* 'Roseum') is commonly planted in northern areas and produces a show of many round clusters of sterile flowers in late spring. Since the snowball effect is produced by conversion of all of its flowers to the showy, sterile type, there is no fruit in autumn. Another bad feature of this popular form is its unusual attractiveness to leaf-feeding aphids, which by their secretions cause the foliage to become malformed and discolored. A more useful plant is a cultivar of European cranberry bush (*Viburnum opulus* 'Xanthocarpum') with fruits that ripen clear yellow, contrasting with the deep green foliage in late summer and autumn. One of the most impressive of all the cranberry bushes is the Susquehanna cranberry bush (*Viburnum sargentii* 'Susquehanna'), a selection released some years ago by the U.S. National Arboretum. This vigorous shrub grows rapidly to 10–15 feet or more in both height and spread, with unusually heavy branches and foliage. Its fruit passes through a long yellow-orange phase in summer before ripening bright red in autumn, and persists long into winter. In early trials, it appears to be hardy in much of northern New England, in areas where winter temperatures regularly fall below −20°F, and it may prove still hardier as further trials are made.

On balance, American cranberry bush and its relatives are among the most functional of large shrubs for cold climates, with colorful flowers, fruit, and autumn foliage, few serious pest problems, and virtual freedom from maintenance. And the cultivars available offer a wide range of seasonal interest and growth rates.

Deciduous
Azaleas

DECIDUOUS AZALEAS ARE AMONG THE MOST COLORFUL of all flowering shrubs, with hundreds of cultivars available in many flower colors. Those of us who live in cold climates are tempted to dismiss azaleas as plants for the South, but a surprising number of them grow well where winter temperatures commonly reach −20°F. Among the showiest are the flame azalea (*Rhododendron calendulaceum*), the Japanese azalea (*R. japonicum*), and a few hybrid groups descended from those species and others.

Visitors to the southern Appalachians in late May have seen the bright orange or yellow flowers of flame azalea in woodland borders. Even though this shrub grows wild only as far north as Pennsylvania, it is cold-hardy enough for much of New England, New York, and Michigan, where annual minimum temperatures average −15°F to −20°F.

Flame azalea grows 8 feet high or more and nearly that wide. The flowers are about 2 inches across and bloom in late May or early June in the North. Unlike flowers of some of the native northern azaleas, such as roseshell (also known in New England as mountain pink, *R. prinophyllum*), those of flame azalea are not fragrant, but they are more showy, with a greater range of color.

Flame azalea is a parent of some of the hardiest of the Ghent hybrid azaleas. This group includes tender cultivars as well, and even the hardiest are not quite so tolerant of cold as the flame azalea parent. Before selecting cultivars, try to find out which have been most successful in your area. A few that have done well in cold climates are: 'Beauté Celeste' (orange-red); 'Charlemagne' (orange); 'Daviesii' (pale yellow, fading to white); 'Gloria Mundi' (red-orange); 'Ignaeum Novum' (orange); 'Narcissiflorum' (clear yellow); 'Pallas' (orange-red); and 'Unique' (yellow-orange).

Japanese azalea is an Asian counterpart of flame azalea, similar in

56

many ways but smaller, usually not exceeding about 6 feet in height and width. Its flowers are larger, 2 to 3 inches across, and borne in larger clusters, with a color range from yellow through orange to red-orange. Unlike those of flame azalea, the flowers of Japanese azalea are scented, but not pleasantly enough to be called fragrant.

Japanese azalea is probably the hardiest of all large-flowered azaleas, thriving in climates where annual minimum temperatures average −20°F to −25°F, but hardiness varies with place of origin. The species grows wild from northern to southern Japan, and plants native to southern Japan are probably less cold-hardy than those from the north.

More common than the wild variety of Japanese azalea are the Molle hybrids. These are the result of crosses with the more tender Chinese azalea (R. *molle*), and include cultivars varying greatly in hardiness. A few of them, including the once-popular 'Miss Louisa Hunnewell,' are about as cold-hardy as the Japanese azalea parent.

In recent years, Molle hybrid azaleas have been largely replaced by Exbury and Knap Hill hybrids, the result of efforts of a number of plant breeders in England and New Zealand. These are hybrids of different cultivars in the Ghent and Molle hybrid groups, their parents, and a few other azalea species. They show a great range of colors and are probably the most important group of deciduous azaleas today in areas where minimum temperatures do not regularly fall below −20°F. Only a few are readily available in any particular place, and experimentation is still going on to determine the exact limits of hardiness of different cultivars. Knap Hill seedlings are sometimes offered for sale instead of cultivars, because propagation by seeds is easier and cheaper than by cuttings, but such seedlings are variable in flower color and hardiness. They should be planted in cold areas only experimentally, but some are turning out to be very fine plants, and, of course, each is a genetic original.

The Northern Lights hybrids, developed by plant breeders at the University of Minnesota Landscape Arboretum, are the best news in many years for residents of really cold climates. These azaleas are grown from seed produced from controlled crosses between a Molle hybrid and a roseshell. The Molle hybrid has contributed large flowers; the roseshell azalea, delightful fragrance and extreme cold-hardiness. Flower buds of the resulting hybrids are said to be hardy to −45°F, and the plants grow to about the same size as Japanese azalea. These hybrids were released only in 1979, so availability may be limited for a few years, but they promise to make a great contribution to far northern landscapes.

Always remember that deciduous azaleas, as well as other members of the Heath family, require acidic soil and a fairly reliable supply of moisture. Any reasonable effort to provide the right conditions will be amply repaid at flowering time.

57

Red Osier
Dogwood

FROM NORTHERN NEW ENGLAND AND NEW YORK through the northern lake states, one of the sad facts of life is that flowering dogwood is, at best, marginally hardy. Unfortunate as that is, it should not obscure the good news that there are at least eight other native species of dogwood, most of which are fine, functional landscape plants adapted to northern as well as southern areas. One of the best landscape plants in this group is red osier dogwood (*Cornus sericea*, also called *C. stolonifera*), a splendid screening shrub with year-round color, beginning with flat sprays of small, white flowers in early summer; bluish white berries, appealing to birds, in late summer; red-to-russet autumn foliage; and bright red twigs that carry color throughout the winter and early spring.

Red osier is a common sight in wet fields and pastures in the northeastern United States, and has a remarkable additional range: from Labrador to the Yukon, southward to California and Arizona in the West, and through the Appalachians in the East. It is not surprising that some plants are hardier than others, and that the hardier varieties easily withstand temperatures of −40°F and lower.

This 6- to 8-foot shrub is most useful in the landscape for visual screening between outdoor areas, or for massing on banks or road-cuts. It is especially well adapted to wet soils, and usually grows wild in wet sites. But when cultivated, it grows well in almost any soil, wet or dry, making it one of the most widely adapted of ornamental shrubs. Because it spreads by occasional rooting-down of prostrate stems, it quickly forms large masses. If it is to be used as a single specimen, it may require pruning to stay within bounds.

Two cultivars of red osier dogwood are worth knowing about. The cultivar 'Flaviramea' usually called "golden-twig dogwood," lacks the red pigment that normally gives twigs and autumn leaves their red color. Because of this, its winter twigs are bright yellow. This color is especially effective when the shrub is planted with a dark background of evergreens, or beside a pond or stream, where blue sky reflection can provide a contrasting background.

A second distinctive cultivar is Kelsey dwarf dogwood, a low-growing (to 2 feet) form of red osier dogwood, useful as a ground cover or for massing in other situations. A word of caution: this cultivar is significantly less hardy than most plants of the species, occasionally showing winter injury in areas where temperatures fall no lower than −20°F, if snow cover is not deep enough to offer protection. And while the idea of a dwarf version of the colorful red osier dogwood is an attractive prospect, it must be admitted that twigs of this cultivar are not nearly so colorful as those of full-size plants.

A close relative from Asia, Tatarian dogwood (*Cornus alba*), is almost indistinguishable from red osier dogwood, except that it is less inclined to spread. This makes it more suitable for use as a specimen, but less desirable for mass plantings. When you want plants to serve as individual specimens, not straying out of bounds, select Tatarian dogwood. But when you want plants to form a thicket quickly, or to have the unique winter interest of the golden-twigged variety, choose red osier dogwood, or its cultivar 'Flaviramea.' If none of these factors is important, the two species can be considered interchangeable.

The most economical way to establish plantings is by bare-root planting in early spring or just at leaf-fall in autumn. But plants can be moved at any time of year when the ground is not frozen, if dug with a soil ball. The landowner with wild thickets on his property and the patience to wait a little longer for results can do it even more economically by propagating plants from hardwood cuttings. Make twig cuttings 12 to 18 inches long as soon as frost is out of the ground in early spring. Treat the lower end of each cutting with a strong preparation of a rooting hormone such as Hormodin or Rootone. Insert the cuttings, right end up, into a bed of well-prepared garden soil, about 16 inches deep, and soak the bed thoroughly. Two years later, at the same season, dig the rooted cuttings and move them to their permanent location. Usually 30 to 80 percent of the cuttings started in this manner can be expected to survive, so plant more than you will actually need. If you are lucky enough to have a surplus of plants later, share them with your neighbors.

59

Roseshell Azalea

AZALEAS IN THE MOUNTAINS OF NEW ENGLAND? A strange thought to some, but no surprise to residents of the Green Mountains of Vermont, who for years have occasionally transplanted seedlings of the native "mountain pink" into their yards. The plant given that descriptive local name is, indeed, an azalea—more widely called roseshell azalea or, botanically, *Rhododendron prinophyllum*. (Both rhododendrons and azaleas belong to the genus *Rhododendron*.) This plant is also listed in some nursery catalogues as *Azalea rosea* or *Rhododendron roseum*. (The latter until recently was the accepted botanical name.) Under any of these names, it is one of the hardiest of all azaleas as well as one of the most delightful, with fragrant, showy flowers during the last days of spring.

With the exception of the rhodora (*Rhododendron canadense*) of far-northern swamps, roseshell azalea is the most northern wild azalea in the Northeast, growing in all of the New England states except Maine. Its range extends about halfway down the Appalachians, then westward to southern Illinois and Missouri.

Under ideal conditions, roseshell azalea may grow above eye level, but usually it remains low. Even when tall, it is not dense enough to make a visual screen. Its soft blue-green foliage contrasts with the brighter greens of other shrubs in mixed plantings. But it is the delightfully scented, clear rose-pink flowers opening just before new leaves emerge that give this plant its greatest appeal.

Like many other shrubs, roseshell azalea can be grown in many places where it is not native, given at least moderately acidic, well-drained soil and cool, temperate climate. Plants native to the northern parts of the range are hardy *at least* to average annual minimum temperatures of −25°F to −30°F, making them adaptable in all the northern states with the possible exception of northern Maine and New Hampshire, northeastern Vermont, and northern Wisconsin and Minnesota.

Before deciding to plant azaleas, it is a good idea to have the planting soil tested for acidity, since correcting improper acidity can be expensive and inconvenient. In most states, soil tests, as well as information on soil preparation, planting, and fertilizing, can be obtained through county offices of the cooperative extension service. Soil that is sufficiently acidic for good growth of blueberries is satisfactory for azaleas. This means a soil pH below 6.0, and preferably below 5.5. Soils of higher pH (less acidic) frequently contain free limestone. When such soils are acidified, the limestone will soon neutralize the acidifying agent, returning the soil to its original pH. Many soils contain enough free limestone to resist artificial acidification for many years.

Even when acidification of the native soil is impractical, the determined gardener still can grow azaleas by making a planting bed 6 to 8 inches above the existing soil level with railroad ties or other retainers, and filling it with a mixture of sand and organic material such as wood chips, sawdust, and acid peat moss. In addition to providing a properly acidic root zone, such raised planting beds insure thorough drainage of excess water, but they also dry out faster, requiring more frequent irrigation during prolonged dry periods. Furthermore, when native soil contains free limestone, the same may hold true for well water from the same area. When lime-free soil mixtures are irrigated with such water, limestone dissolved in the water is precipitated and held in the soil, accumulating until the substitute soil is just as unfavorable for azalea roots as the native soil that it replaced. If all this seems discouraging, it may be of some comfort to New England gardeners that most soils there are sufficiently acidic for azaleas without modification.

Even though roseshell azaleas have been transplanted from the wild in the past, it probably is not a good idea now, for reasons of conservation and because of the difficulties involved. This plant is listed by only a few nurseries in the New England area, but is sold by some additional nurseries under the name of its close relative, the pinxterbloom azalea (*Rhododendron periclymenoides* or *R. nudiflorum*), which has paler, scentless flowers and is less hardy. When available, roseshell azalea is the preferred choice, under whatever name it can be found.

Roseshell azalea also has been used in hybridization by plant breeders in cold climates. The late Frank Abbott of Saxton's River, Vermont, has produced hardy seedlings, more showy than their roseshell parent, under the collective name "Jane Abbott." University of Minnesota plant breeders have crossed roseshell azalea with one of the large-flowered Molle hybrid azaleas, with results that are promising. Meanwhile, the roseshell azalea offers a combination of hardiness and fragrant, rose-pink flowers that makes it an asset to any northern garden.

Summersweet

BEFORE
PRUNING

AFTER
PRUNING

NEW
GROWTH

SHRUBS THAT PROVIDE FLOWERING INTEREST IN SUMMER bear a premium in any climate, but especially in northern areas where spring-flowering shrubs often fail to bloom because of winter killing of dormant flower buds or spring freezing of opening flowers. When you look among summer-flowering shrubs for those that also are tolerant of wet sites, the list becomes very short. One of the best of these is summersweet (*Clethra alnifolia*), a native of much of the eastern United States.

Summersweet is a rather large shrub at maturity, tall enough and dense enough to serve as a visual screen, but also useful as a specimen for accent, as a component of a mixed shrub border, or even in mass plantings designed to remain below eye level, since its height can be controlled easily by pruning. It also has been used effectively as a formal hedge, but inevitably with some loss of its unique character.

The name summersweet comes from this shrub's primary seasonal interest—fragrant, small, white (or pink) flowers, borne in large numbers in spikelike clusters to 6 inches long. Since they open progressively, from bottom to top of the cluster, they remain colorful for as long as three weeks in midsummer.

The foliage of this plant offers further seasonal interest. In summer it is dark green, lustrous, and neat in texture. In autumn it turns yellow-orange—colorful in good years, less so in others.

Summersweet, which is sometimes called sweet pepperbush, is native to some of the colder parts of the Northeast, and it is reasonable to

62

expect that shrubs of northern origin should be fully hardy in all of New England, and in all of the Lake States except possibly northern Minnesota. This may not be true for plants originating in native stands in the South Atlantic area, however.

Clethra alnifolia belongs to a small family (Clethraceae) closely allied with the Heath family (Ericaceae), which includes rhododendrons, blueberries, and other acid-soil plants. So it is not surprising that *Clethra* is a poor choice for high-limestone soils, although it may be more lime-tolerant than some of the other acid-soil plants. It grows wild in both swamps and sandy woods, and in cultivation will tolerate both wet and moderately dry soils, but, as Donald Wyman has pointed out in *Shrubs and Vines for American Gardens* (Macmillan, New York, 1969), dry soil increases its susceptibility to infestation by red mites.

In general, summersweet can be considered a low-maintenance plant. The problem of mites can be largely avoided by restricting its use to sites where the moisture supply is fairly reliable. At present, it has few other insect or disease problems. Also in the interest of low maintenance, this plant will stay full and shapely for several years with little or no pruning. Old plants can become leggy, eventually requiring renewal pruning. This can be done by removing a few of the oldest main branches close to ground level each year, gradually allowing old, leggy branches to be replaced with young, vigorous ones over a period of three or more years. Or, the courageous gardener can cut down the entire top of a healthy, overgrown plant in a single operation, and let the whole shrub renew itself at once. Drastic as this practice sounds, it is reasonably safe except in areas where the plant is marginally hardy. It is crucial, though, that such drastic pruning be done in spring, to allow maximum time for growth and acclimation of the new tops before winter. The practice of heading-back with hedge shears should be avoided, generally, unless a formal hedge is intended. Some selective heading-back of individual shoots may be desirable along with renewal pruning, but this should be done with great restraint.

Another advantage of summersweet in some areas is its ability to grow in the presence of salt. It grows wild close to the seashore, and has proved adaptable to seaside planting as well. Its salt tolerance there suggests tolerance of road de-icing salts as well, but it would be a mistake to assume that it will tolerate the most severe salt conditions that exist near roads and salted walks during northern winters, since so few plants can.

Even though summersweet typically has white flowers, a pink-flowered form discovered about seventy years ago gradually has found its way into the nursery trade. It is now available as the cultivar 'Rosea.' Except for flower color, it is similar to the white-flowered type, but it has called renewed attention to this excellent shrub, which still remains unnoticed by all but a small segment of the gardening public.

Winged Euonymus

LANDSCAPE PLANTS THAT ARE INTERESTING in all seasons are always at a premium, especially if their feature of interest changes seasonally. One notable example of such a plant is winged euonymus (*Euonymus alata*), also called winged spindletree and burning-bush.

Originally from northeastern Asia, this shrub is equally at home in the climate of much of temperate North America and has even escaped cultivation to become naturalized in a few places. It is hardy enough to withstand the cold in northern New England and North Dakota and northern Minnesota—areas where minimum temperatures average lower than − 30°F, and occasionally reach − 40°F.

Winged euonymus makes an excellent hedge, tall enough to serve as a visual screen if desired. Left unpruned, it remains full and symmetrical, or it can be shaped into a formal hedge with only a single annual clipping in early summer. Hardy and able to tolerate winds, it grows well when planted by the corners of buildings, but its ultimate height of 10 feet is out of scale with buildings of less than two stories.

The most showy feature of winged euonymus is its brilliant autumnal foliage. As the scarlet or fiery brick red leaves gradually fade to shades of delicate pink, the plant can be a delightful sight in a backyard corner. But what appears as a striking splash of color in an informal autumnal setting can be discordant in a more natural one, so it is important to consider the nature of the landscape when deciding where to use this plant.

64

When the foliage falls in autumn, the small, bright red fruits become much more apparent, and provide color for several more weeks. But it is the bare twigs with their unusual corky wings that provide continuing interest. The wings give the twigs an appearance unmatched by any other plant, varying from the warm brown, crisp branching pattern seen on sunny winter days, to the dripping, rain-darkened twigs of drizzly days, to the spectral quality of twigs sheathed in ice following freezing rains.

When buds open in spring, the pale green leaves and stems combine with the older winged twigs to form a lacy pattern of brown and soft green. As the leaves mature in summer they turn a darker green and remain crisp, clean, and handsome until autumnal color returns once more.

The most important limitation of winged euonymus in landscaping is its size. Full-grown plants typically reach heights of about 10 feet, and they are equally broad. In small-scale situations, you can control the size somewhat by pruning, but a better solution is to select a different shrub, one that will remain the appropriate size without such persuasion.

There is a cultivar, called 'Compacta,' that grows more slowly and remains more compact than ordinary winged euonymus for several years, but eventually even this "compact" shrub will reach heights of 8 feet or more. Since all plants of 'Compacta' are propagated by cuttings, they constitute a clone; thus they are genetically identical, with a uniform growth rate, form, and foliage color, given uniform soil and environment. When planting a formal hedge, 'Compacta' (or some other clone) is more likely to give the desired uniformity than any group of seedling plants.

In addition to its compact form and slower growth, 'Compacta' has foliage that turns early and displays unusually brilliant color—striking as an accent in a formal garden but too strong for more informal or natural situations. Its twigs are narrowly winged, so they are less interesting in winter than those of typical winged euonymus. Finally, plants of 'Compacta' have shown winter dieback in areas where typical plants of winged euonymus are hardy, so their use should be limited to localities where winter temperatures seldom drop below −20°F.

'Compacta' probably has overtaken ordinary winged euonymus as a commercial landscaping plant, but it is unlikely that it will replace it. Clearly, there is a place for each. When deciding which to use, consider space limitations, growth rate, and need for uniformity. But also remember to consider the value of broadly winged twigs in the winter landscape, the intensity of foliage color, and, above all, hardiness. With such a thoughtful approach to selection, whichever type you finally choose will be functional, durable, and a broadly interesting addition to the landscape.

Winterberry Holly

HOLLY IN THE NORTHERN LANDSCAPE? Yes, if your idea of holly is broad enough to include deciduous types. The familiar spiny-leaved evergreen hollies are mostly restricted to climates where winter temperatures do not regularly drop below − 10°F, and many will barely tolerate zero cold. But the deciduous holly called winterberry (*Ilex verticillata*) survives in the North Country where, as a wild plant in swamps, it is also called black alder. Even though it is not evergreen, this thick-forming shrub provides outstanding seasonal color during late autumn and early winter.

Winterberry is native to a large part of eastern North America, from Newfoundland to Minnesota and southward to northern Georgia and northeastern Texas. As with all such wide-ranging shrubs and trees, plants of northern origin should be used for landscape planting in the North, and southern plants in the South.

In most of its native habitat, winterberry is a shrub reaching heights of 8 to 10 feet, but under ideal conditions in the South it may become almost treelike, reaching 15 feet. When growing vigorously in full sun, it sends up many suckers and eventually spreads into a large thicket. This tendency to produce suckers can be a problem in mixed shrub borders, but it is easily controlled when this species is used by itself—for massing or screening.

Even though winterberry tolerates wet soils, it will grow just as well in good soil of average moisture content. Whether wet or not, the soil should be somewhat acidic for good growth and foliage color, testing no higher than pH 6. This shrub will grow well in partial shade, but should receive full sun for at least half the day for best fruiting.

Winterberry is not a plant with broad seasonal interest. Its foliage is medium green and not striking, turning black after the first hard frost in early autumn, and its flowers are visible but hardly conspicuous. But when the leaves have fallen, the shiny, brilliant red fruits are left fully exposed to shine like small clusters of jewels on the gray twigs. From October until December, there is no more colorful sight in northern landscapes.

But now for a sobering note. Winterberry is a dioecious shrub: that is, male and female flowers are borne on separate plants. Only female plants will bear fruits, and the occasional male plant must be nearby for pollination of the fruiting females. The usual way to obtain maximum fruiting is to include a male plant in a mass planting of up to five or six females. The nonfruiting male may be set at the rear of the planting, reserving more prominent positions for the colorful females.

In northern areas where winterberry grows wild, it is an old custom to cut berry-laden stems in early December to serve as holiday decorations. This practice was more successful before the advent of central heat, for once brought indoors, winterberry fruits do not remain colorful for long in the dry air caused by modern heating. The practice is questionable for another reason: winterberry usually is not found in large stands and can easily be depleted by too much cutting. In locations where winterberry occupies a prominent place, it may be more community-minded to leave the plants intact for viewing by all, at the same time helping to guarantee similar shows in future years.

Individual plants that display outstanding fruiting have been selected and propagated vegetatively (by cuttings) to maintain their special character, but these are seldom available in nurseries. A relatively new selection called 'Winter Red,' introduced by an Indiana nursery, Simpson Orchard Company of Vincennes, promises to become more widely available and is well worth seeking out for its heavy and long-lasting display of fruit. It is not yet known whether this selection is as cold-hardy as wild plants from the extreme North, but it seems safe in areas having minimum temperatures of −20°F to −25°F, and it may prove hardier still. As with any other female winterberry, it needs the presence of a male for pollination.

Usually trouble free, winterberry occasionally is affected by mites and leaf-spot diseases. None of these problems requires corrective action except in small-scale situations where the affected foliage is unattractive at close range. Pruning is needed only when it is desirable to remove suckers, or to renew old plants. With minimum care, winterberry functions effectively in wet soils and provides outstanding landscape color at an otherwise colorless season.

DECIDUOUS TALL SHRUBS AND SMALL TREES (12 to 24 feet tall) VI

THIS GROUP INCLUDES TALL SCREENING SHRUBS, garden and patio trees, and a few plants, including Amur maple, black haw, and Russian-olive, that can be trained to function in either way.

In some situations, visual screens must be taller than the 6 to 12 feet provided by medium shrubs. Land on one side of the screen may be elevated, requiring a higher barrier, or privacy may be needed on a raised deck. Whenever extra height is needed, shrubs in this group are especially useful.

Small trees, especially those with distinctive seasonal interest, are always in great demand. They can be used under power lines by streets and highways, or located in intensively used areas of the landscape where their seasonal interest will be appreciated often and at close range.

The tall shrubs and small trees that follow are not an all-inclusive listing, but include many of the best in this group for cold climates.

Amur Maple

FEW TREES ARE AS WELL KNOWN IN THE NORTHEAST as sugar maple, few as little known as Amur maple (*Acer ginnala*). Yet Amur maple is a particularly useful landscape tree in the coldest areas of the northeastern and north central U.S. Since it remains small, it complements rather than duplicates the landscape function of sugar maple. And it equals sugar maple in autumn brilliance.

Amur maple takes its name from one of the places where it grows wild: the region of the Amur River, which forms part of the boundary between Manchuria and Siberia. Having become adapted to the sharp cold waves that pass over this region from northern Siberia, it is suited to similar climates in North America.

A typical Amur maple leaf has a middle lobe much longer than those at each side, unlike leaves of more familiar maples. While this lends a distinctive appearance, it is not a sure means of identification, since leaves of a few other maples, such as Tatarian maple, also have elongated central lobes.

In landscape use, Amur maple starts with a shrubby, indefinite form, later developing into a broad, round-topped tree with a short trunk, usually branching close to the ground. It seldom grows taller than 20 feet, which is an asset in small-scale situations. Even though it is not as graceful as Japanese maple, its denseness, fine branching, and general form recommend it as a substitute in areas too cold for Japanese maple, such as northern New England. It also can serve as an effective visual screen in summer, if lightly pruned to keep it full at the base or sheared into a formal hedge.

The fragrant, pale yellow flowers emerge along with those of flowering crabapples, later than those of most maples. In clusters they are not striking, but offer quiet landscape interest. Reddish fruits (samaras) follow in midsummer. On some trees they are bright scarlet, offering striking landscape interest. Summer transplanting is not recommended, but when buying a tree from a local nursery, it may be possible to select one with colorful fruits in summer for later transplanting. Nurseries would be more interested in perpetuating outstanding color variants if vegetative propagation of such forms were less difficult and costly. With continued improvements in propagation techniques, named varieties with outstanding fruit color may become available in the future.

This tree's greatest landscape show comes in autumn, when its foliage turns from dark green to scarlet. Some trees are more brilliant than others, and intensity of color varies from year to year, but few species present a more reliable display of color in the fall.

Fortunately, very little maintenance is required beyond normal care in transplanting. Insects and diseases are seldom serious problems, and pruning is largely unnecessary unless one wants to train the plant into a particular form. Its leaves and fruits do not make much litter in autumn, and its branches are not particularly prone to storm damage.

Amur maple will grow in almost any soil found in the Northeast. It grows better than most maples in moderately dry soil, and more rapidly yet with optimal moisture. Like most maples (native red and silver maples excluded), it does not perform well on very wet or poorly drained soils.

Usually it is better to purchase well-started trees than to wait out the slow early growth of seedlings. Nursery-grown trees that must be dug from the ground can be moved in early spring or early autumn, except in the extreme North, where fall planting can be risky. Container-grown trees can be transplanted at any time from early spring through early summer. Such plants have received near-optimal amounts of fertilizer and water in the nursery, and so have not developed extensive roots. Even though roots are not lost in transplanting, these plants must grow a much larger root system before they are able to cope with the relatively dry conditions of a landscape site, and this takes time. Late summer or fall planting can be risky since it cuts short the available adjustment time before winter.

Even though Amur maple is not a common maple, it can be found in many nurseries in the Northeast and Midwest. For an extremely hardy, reliably small tree with intense scarlet autumn color and a pleasing appearance at other seasons, it is a happy choice.

71

Arrowwood

IT TAKES A STRONG SUPPORTING CAST, in most plays, to bring out the best performance of the leading players. The same principle is true for landscape plants. For every attention-getting plant, many more neutral plants are needed to provide background against which the accent plant can be fully appreciated. There is probably no better shrub for neutral massing and screening than arrowwood (*Viburnum dentatum*). But in a restrained way it also provides interest of its own.

Arrowwood is native to most of the eastern United States and adjacent Canada. The extreme northern form, separated by some botanists as *Viburnum recognitum*, is scarcely different from a landscape viewpoint. The two types may as well be considered interchangeable, as they have indeed been interchanged in usage for years. Plants originally cultivated from southern seed sources are probably not well adapted to very cold climates, nor those from northern sources to climates of the Deep South, There is little direct evidence of this, but virtually every wide-ranging woody plant species studied to date has shown great variation in adaptation, and arrowwood is probably no exception.

Arrowwood grows to 10 feet or more in height, taller in shaded sites. In full sun it is compact and rounded, the branches arching somewhat with age. The base of the plant is kept full by a progression of sucker shoots arising from the rootstock. These shoots grow rapidly and are often straight enough to serve as arrow shafts, probably the reason for the common name.

This shrub's own seasonal interest begins in late spring, with the appearance of creamy white flowers in clusters 2 inches or more across.

72

The dark green, sometimes lustrous, sharp-toothed leaves provide an attractive neutral foliage mass until autumn, when they sometimes turn bright maroon or even scarlet before falling. Small berries replace the flowers in clusters, ripening dark blue in late summer. They provide color contrast with the reddening autumn foliage until they are taken by birds.

Arrowwood is most often used as a visual screen or background for more showy plants. In a mixed shrub border it combines well with other plants, adding its own distinctive interest. Over the wide area where it is native it is an appropriate choice for naturalizing, and it can be preserved where it is found growing wild.

One of the most valued features of this shrub is its adaptability. When appropriate seed sources are used, it will tolerate annual minimum temperatures that average − 25°F and lower. Moreover, it grows well in sunny and shady sites, even though flowering and fruiting are reduced in deep shade. Arrowwood is also widely tolerant of soil conditions, growing well in soil that is moderately dry or wet, over a range of acidity so wide that it seldom limits the plant's performance. Add to this a considerable salt-tolerance (for a viburnum) and the result is a shrub that is seldom limited by site conditions in the north-central and northeastern United States.

A few close relatives of arrowwood inhabit woodlands of eastern North America, and are potentially useful landscape plants. Downy arrowwood (*Viburnum rafinesquianum*), native from Quebec to Manitoba and southward to Georgia and Illinois, is a slightly smaller shrub than arrowwood, less reliable for screening but otherwise similar as a landscape plant.

Mapleleaf viburnum (*Viburnum acerifolium*), also called dockmackie, is a weaker-growing shrub, seldom reaching above eye level, and seems to require at least partial shade to grow well. Its main advantage is its tolerance of deep shade and its maplelike leaves, which turn deep purple in autumn.

One of the most impressive of the native viburnums in flower is hobblebush (*Viburnum alnifolium*), a rangy shrub that is tall enough but not dense enough to make an effective screen. Like mapleleaf viburnum, it grows best with some shade from full sun. Its usefulness is limited to natural or naturalized landscapes, where its white flowers are showy even from a distance in late May. Its large, rounded, downy leaves, vaguely reminiscent of those of basswood, turn to a beautiful wine red in autumn, giving it two distinct seasons of color.

Whether the need is for background, screening, or naturalizing, arrowwood and other native viburnums contribute color and interest of their own, without visually overwhelming other plants. This and their wide adaptability suggest that they could well be used more than they are at present.

Black Haw

BLACK HAW (*Viburnum prunifolium*) is one of the most interesting and versatile of all native shrubs. It is broadly adapted to eastern North America, remains interesting throughout the leafy season, and can be used either as a visual screen or as a small patio tree. In spite of its virtues, however, it is not widely used.

The word *haw* refers to the fruit of certain shrubs and trees, primarily hawthorns (*Crataegus* species). This viburnum probably was first called black haw because of its nearly black fruits and twiggy growth, reminiscent of a hawthorn.

Black haw grows wild from Connecticut and Michigan southward to Florida and Texas, and it has been adapted to cultivation considerably farther north, even in areas where annual minimum temperatures average −35°F and occasionally fall to −45°F. That makes it cold-hardy in the entire eastern half of the United States, except perhaps for the northernmost parts of Minnesota. But satisfactory performance in the Far North, and probably in the South as well, depends on the use of plants having their origin in the same general region where they are to be planted.

As its broad natural range suggests, black haw is adaptable to a variety of soils and exposures. It must have reasonably well-drained soil to perform well, but is tolerant of moderate periods of drought. It flowers and fruits best in full sun, but will grow in almost complete shade.

The small white flowers of black haw, borne in flattened clusters, are reasonably showy as they open in late spring. The foliage expands during flowering, turns deep green and lustrous during the summer, then becomes red-purple to bright crimson in midautumn. The large berries form in late summer, briefly turning yellowish white before ripening to blue-black in autumn, making an interesting contrast with the red foliage. The edible fruits are attractive to birds and can be made into preserves.

Black haw is truly striking only when it's in flower and when the leaves turn in autumn, but it is interesting in all seasons. The stiffly upright, twiggy form lends itself well to training into a small, upright tree, seldom exceeding 15 feet in height. Without such training, black haw forms a dense, low-branching shrub that makes an excellent visual screen by itself or as part of a mixed shrub border. It does not grow rapidly (it increases in height by less than a foot each year in most sites), but its longevity and freedom from maintenance are impressive, making it a most attractive choice where instant effect is not needed.

Transplanting nursery-grown plants is not difficult, but best results can be obtained by digging all but the smallest plants with a soil ball, or by using container-grown plants. Transplanting wild plants from the woods is quite difficult—probably an exercise in futility for those with no experience. Even nursery experts find that propagation of cuttings is a more foolproof and economical route to production of salable plants.

Another native viburnum, closely related and similar to black haw in most ways, should be considered for alternative planting in some situations. This plant, nannyberry (*Viburnum lentago*), has a more northerly native distribution—to Hudson Bay and Manitoba—yet grows wild as far south as northern Georgia and Mississippi. If plants of nearby origin are used, nannyberry can be grown in areas where annual minimum temperatures average −40°F or lower, so it is adaptable to the coldest areas in the United States and most of eastern Canada.

Nannyberry grows at least as tall as black haw, occasionally 25 to 30 feet, but is not so easily trained into a single-trunked tree, since it produces many root suckers. Its branches are more arching and its overall aspect more informal than black haw's, but otherwise the two are so similar they are sometimes confused. In summer, nannyberry is easily recognized by the wavy margin of tissue along the sides of the leaf petiole.

Both of these viburnums are usually trouble free, although mildew can be a problem in sites that are shaded or have poor air circulation, especially in southern areas. Both black haw and nannyberry are serviceable large shrubs or small trees with landscape interest during most of the year. Both are native plants that need little maintenance, and they remain functional and handsome in the landscape for many years.

Flowering Crabapples

FLOWERING CRABAPPLES (*Malus* species and cultivars) are the most widely used of all flowering trees in cold climates. In fact, they have become so popular that the number of cultivars now available is in the hundreds, and the wide selection can make it difficult to choose the best crabapple for a particular landscape use.

Most modern flowering crabapples are not wild species but complex hybrids developed by crossing several species. Often the wild ancestors of cultivars are not known, so many varieties cannot be identified as members of a species group and have to be evaluated separately. That keeps crabapple specialists busy obtaining, sorting, and disseminating current information. Up-to-date evaluations of old and new crabapples in specific regions can be obtained through cooperative extension services in most states.

Crabapples in blossom are beautiful to behold. In midspring (May in New England), the trees bloom with a rich array of whites, pinks, and various shades of rose to deep red. Almost any flowering crabapple will be spectacular in a good year. Knowing that, you can place more emphasis on other important selection criteria.

Cold-hardiness Most crabapples are relatively cold-hardy, but there are important differences among them. A few, such as Hall crabapple (*Malus halliana*) and Oregon crabapple (*M. fusca*), will tolerate temperatures only as low as −10°F to −15°F, while others, such as Siberian crabapple (*M. baccata*) and the cultivar 'Dolgo,' are perfectly hardy to −35°F or lower. Residents of cold climates who fail to consider such variations may be disappointed by trees that can't survive the winter.

Size and shape Flowering crabapples vary in mature size from the Sargent crabapple (*M. sargentii*), which hardly ever exceeds 8 or 10 feet in height but spreads to 25 or 30 feet in width, to Siberian crabapple, some forms of which grow as tall as 40 feet. A few crabapples, such as 'Red Jade,' have strongly pendulous branches. Others, such as 'Beauty,' columnar Siberian crabapple (*M. baccata* 'Columnaris'), and 'Royalty,' are definitely upright in habit. A few are unique: Tea crabapple (*M. hupehensis*), for example, is an upright and vase-shaped tree, with sparsely distributed, picturesquely twisting branches.

Disease resistance Some of the best known and most frequently used crabapples, such as 'Almey,' carmine crabapple (*M.* x *atrosanguinea*) 'Eleyi,' and 'Hopa,' are among the most susceptible to disease. That is an obvious problem at a time when use of chemicals to control disease and pests is being reduced on all fronts because of concern for personal safety and environmental quality. Fortunately, more information on disease resistance is available now than ever before, and most of the recently introduced crabapples are distinctly superior to their predecessors.

Annual bloom Many crabapples flower heavily only in alternate years. The reason is that fruit formation after flowering competes with formation of flower buds for the next year. But not all cultivars show that tendency; some flower heavily every year, and so offer an advantage over those that don't.

Fruiting interest Some crabapples, especially those with double flowers such as Bechtel's crabapple (*M. ioensis* 'Plena'), have little or no fruiting interest. A few, such as 'Beauty' and 'Dolgo,' have large fruit that are good for jelly making but have only a transitory landscape effect. Others, such as the redbud flowering crabapple (*M.* x *zumi* 'Calocarpa'), 'Bob White,' and 'Indian Magic,' have small red or yellow fruits that remain colorful throughout autumn and in some cases well into winter. One of the most active originators of new cultivars, Robert Simpson of Vincennes, Indiana, has stressed development of cultivars with strong fruiting interest, and there should be a greater selection of such types in the future.

Foliage interest Foliage quality depends in part on susceptibility to apple scab disease; highly susceptible cultivars are sometimes defoliated before the end of summer. A few crabapples have unusual foliage. 'Royalty' stands out because it has the most intensely purple foliage of any crabapple that is commercially available. Tschonoski crabapple (*M. tschonoskii*) is unique because its leaves are coated with a mat of silvery hairs when young, and they turn yellow, red, or purple in autumn. (But this wild Japanese variety is outstanding only in its foliage interest; its flowers and fruits are insignificant.)

The accompanying chart summarizes some of the most important features of a small number of flowering crabapples that are currently in favor. The list is by no means comprehensive; many other good crabapples are on the market. Always check with local sources for information about local performance and availability.

Characteristics of Some of the Better Flowering Crabapples

Name	Cold-hardy to (°F)	Height (feet)	Growth Habit	Annual (A) or Biennial (B) Flowering and Fruiting	Flowers	Fruit	Susceptible (S) or Resistant (R) to:			Comments
							Scab	Fire-Blight	Rust	
'Adams'	−25	25	Upright and spreading	A	Purple to pink, single	Red, early autumn	R	R	R	More disease resistant than the Rosybloom crabapples
M. baccata 'Columnaris' (Columnar Siberian Crabapple)	−40	40	Upright, narrowly pyramidal	A	White, single, fragrant	Yellow, red blush, autumn and early winter	R(S?)	R	R	Distinctive growth habit
M. baccata 'Jackii' (Jack Siberian Crabapple)	−40	30	Upright and spreading	A	White, single, fragrant	Red, autumn and early winter	R	R	R	Disease resistant
'Bob White'	−25	20	Upright and spreading	B	Rose in bud; white, single, fragrant blossoms	Yellow, autumn and winter	R	R	R	Outstanding fruiting interest
'Dolgo'	−35	35	Upright and spreading	A	White, single	Red, late summer	R	R	R	Dual purpose: jellies
M. floribunda (Japanese Flowering Crabapple)	−20	15–20	Rounded and spreading	A	Rose in bud; pink to white, single blossoms	Yellow, slight red blush, early autumn	R	R(S?)	R	Distinctive flowers
M. hupehensis (Tea Crabapple)	−25	15–20	Upright, vase-shaped, open	B	Deep pink in bud; pale pink to white, single blossoms	Greenish-yellow, red blush, early autumn	R	R(S?)	R	Distinctive growth habit and flowering
'Indian Magic'	−25	20	Upright and spreading	A	Rose, single	Golden-orange, autumn and winter	R	R	R	Outstanding fruiting
M. ioensis 'Plena' (Bechtel Crabapple)	−30	15	Upright and spreading	A	Pink, large, double, fragrant	Greenish, insignificant	R	R	S	Outstanding flowers: clear pink, very late
'Mary Potter'	−25	12–15	Spreading, broad and low	A(B?)	Rose in bud; white, single blossoms	Red, autumn	R	R	R	Similar to M. sargentii, but larger
'Ormiston Roy'	−30	20	Upright and spreading	A	Rose in bud; pink to white, single blossoms	Yellow-orange, flushed red, to early winter	R	R	R	Similar to M. floribunda, but later fruiting
M. x purpurea 'Lemoinei' (Lemoine Purple Crabapple)	−30	25	Upright and spreading	A	Red-purple, single	Purple, late summer	S	R	R	Outstanding in flower
'Red Jade'	−35	10–12	Strongly weeping	A	Pink in bud; white, small blossoms	Brilliant red, autumn	R(S?)	R	R	Distinctive fruiting
'Royalty'	−35	25	Upright and spreading	A	Dull purple, single	Dull purple, autumn	S	R	R	Best red-leaved crabapple
M. sargentii (Sargent Crabapple)	−25	8–10	Broad-spreading, very low	B	Pink in bud; white, single blossoms	Red, autumn	R	R	R	Lowest of all crabapples
M. tschonoskii (Tschonoski Crabapple)	−25	30	Upright	A (few flowers)	White, insignificant	Insignificant	R	R	R	Colorful foliage, summer and autumn
'White Angel'	−25	25	Upright	A	White, single	Red, to early winter	R	R(S?)	R	Outstanding fruiting
M. x zumi 'Calocarpa' (Redbud Flowering Crabapple)	−25	25	Rounded and spreading	B	Pink in bud; white, single blossoms	Red, autumn and winter	R	R	R	Outstanding fruiting

N O T R E E I S M O R E P O P U L A R T H A N F L O W E R I N G D O G W O O D
(*Cornus florida*) in areas where both soil and climate are amenable to
its growth. It is among the most useful of small trees, and one of few
that are interesting in all seasons.

Flowering dogwood grows wild over much of the eastern United
States, from New England to Michigan and southward to Florida and
Texas. Its northern limits reach into southern Maine, New Hampshire,
Vermont, central New York, southern Ontario, and southern Michigan. There is ample evidence that wild trees in those areas, or trees
grown from their seed, are better adapted to cold winters than more
southern natives. Residents of cold climates may protest that flowering
dogwood is not truly hardy, and it is a sad fact that failures with this tree
far outnumber successes in areas much colder than those where it
grows wild. Research has shown that flowering dogwood is already
growing wild in most areas where it is climatically adapted, and we
cannot expect to extend its *useful* range much beyond its *natural* range.
As usual, there are exceptions to that rule, however. Planted dogwoods
from northern seed sources are performing reasonably well in the Lake
Champlain Valley, a hundred miles north of the nearest native stands,
thanks to the lake, which moderates the climate along its shores. Simi-

**Flowering
Dogwood**

79

lar situations exist on the eastern shores of Lake Michigan and Lake Huron.

In some areas nurseries produce dogwood trees from local seed sources for local sale—biologically and horticulturally a sound practice. But great numbers of dogwood trees are produced in southern nurseries from southern seed sources and then shipped to northern areas for retail sale. Trees native to North Carolina or Tennessee may be hardy enough for southern Pennsylvania or Indiana, but they cannot be expected to perform well in places where flowering dogwood approaches its northern limits.

What is it about flowering dogwood that justifies taking extreme measures to use it at the very edge of its range, against long odds? Briefly stated, it is its combination of outstanding usefulness and year-round beauty.

When flowering dogwood is planted next to outdoor sitting areas, its strikingly horizontal branches provide a comfortable feeling of enclosure overhead. The tree never grows too large to be appreciated at close range, yet it is perhaps most beautiful when it is seen in full bloom from a distance, with dark woodland for background.

In midspring—May in the north—the scales that cover the dormant flower buds in winter expand into showy, white, petal-like bracts, unless they have been winterkilled. When injury is marginal, the bracts may not open completely, or only the two inside ones may expand. The cluster of small, greenish yellow flowers at the center of the bracts sometimes survives even when the bracts are killed, in which case fruiting is still possible.

In good fruiting years, dogwood flowers are followed by clusters of berries, which ripen shiny scarlet in early autumn and remain until taken by birds. The handsome green leaves provide background for the fruiting display until they, too, turn red in autumn. They turn dark maroon at first, and finally brilliant crimson before falling. After leaf-fall the horizontally branching and light gray twigs, terminated by buttonlike winter buds, add quiet interest to the landscape all winter.

Several cultivars of flowering dogwood are on the market, some with pink rather than white bracts, a few almost red. Most of the available cultivars have been selected from native trees in the central or southern parts of the range, so they are not suitable for climates where winter temperatures regularly drop far below zero.

Where winter temperatures usually fall to −25°F or lower, attempting to grow flowering dogwood probably is a waste of time. Where winter lows usually run −15°F to −25°F, consider this tree for experimental planting only. If it fails, fall back on the interesting pagoda dogwood (*Cornus alternifolia*) as a substitute. But if flowering dogwood succeeds for you, you will be the proud owner of one of the most colorful and useful of all landscape trees.

HAWTHORNS, OR THORN-APPLES as they are sometimes called, receive their share of disdain where they grow as weed trees in old pastures, and some of them deserve scorn as landscape plants as well. But a few are quite satisfactory small landscape trees, providing distinctive interest with their layered branching, late spring flowers, and, in some cases, lustrous foliage and colorful fruits.

Hawthorns

Cockspur hawthorn (*Crataegus crus-galli*) is a wide-spreading tree native from Quebec to Michigan and southward to North Carolina. It stays under 25 feet in height for many years, but eventually spreads to 40 feet across. Its strikingly horizontal branching is accentuated by white flowers in late spring. This hawthorn's red fruits or haws, about three eighths of an inch across, remain colorful well into early winter unless taken by birds earlier. Even after all color is gone, this tree's twiggy, horizontal branching keeps it interesting, especially when outlined with new snow.

The large thorns of cockspur hawthorn are a potential hazard, especially on trunks and low branches. The thornless selection 'Inermis' might better be used in doubtful situations. Unfortunately, it is not widely available, but its increasing use may make it progressively easier to obtain.

Cockspur hawthorn is not so seriously damaged by cedar-apple rust as some hawthorns, but it is susceptible. This disease is caused by a fungus that can only complete its life cycle by infecting red-cedar (*Juniperus virginiana*), and so is a problem to hawthorns only where red-cedar trees are also present. In areas where winter minimum temperatures normally fall below −25°F, red-cedar is likely to be encountered only when it has been planted, and this disease problem can be solved simply by not planting red-cedar trees in the neighborhood of hawthorns.

Perhaps the most trouble free of all hawthorns is Washington haw- thorn (*Crataegus phaenopyrum*). In spite of its more southern native distribution, from Pennsylvania to Missouri and southward to Florida, it performs well in areas where winter temperatures regularly fall to −20°F. Washington hawthorn has a delicately twiggy growth habit, without the striking horizontal branching of cockspur hawthorn. It reaches about the same height when mature: 25 feet or a bit more, but its spread rarely exceeds its height. Its lower branches are higher than those of cockspur hawthorn, and nurseries usually train it a bit higher still, sometimes to a 5-foot trunk, and remove the large thorns from trunk and lowest branches. For the complete safety of pedestrians pass- ing underneath, thorny branches that sag because of their weight as the tree grows should be removed.

Few trees have a more consistent display of seasonal interest than Washington hawthorn. Its white flowers appear in flattened clusters, displayed effectively against a background of rich green foliage, in late spring or early summer. After flowering, the handsomely textured, lobed leaves remain interesting through the growing season, turning red-orange in autumn in some locations and in some years. The great- est single display is that made by the abundant small, glossy, orange- red fruits, which are showy from early autumn until midwinter.

A third hawthorn has become very popular in the Midwest during recent years. 'Winter King,' a superior clone of green hawthorn (*Cra- taegus viridis*), was selected by Robert Simpson of Vincennes, Indiana, who has also introduced several flowering crabapple cultivars with out- standing fruiting interest. This tree is larger than most hawthorns, to 30 or 35 feet tall. Its orange-red fruits, not so glossy as those of Washing- ton hawthorn but slightly larger, remain colorful at least until midwin- ter, and even later in mild winters. Further winter interest is provided by silvery gray bark on twigs and branches. Bark on trunks of older trees becomes flaky and multicolored. Like other hawthorns, 'Winter King' is interesting in flower in late spring, and its foliage is about as at- tractive as that of Washington hawthorn but less likely to be colorful in autumn. This selection has fewer thorns than either cockspur or Washington hawthorn, but those that remain must be treated with re- spect.

Hardiness of 'Winter King' is not fully known. It appears to be fully cold-hardy where minimum temperatures reach −15°F to −20°F, but until there have been more opportunities for observation in very cold climates, it should be used only experimentally where temperatures frequently drop below −20°F.

These three are among the very best hawthorns that are commer- cially available. Used where they are adapted and given a sunny site in well-drained soil, they make fine small trees with minimal troubles and considerable seasonal interest.

IN THE NORTHERN UNITED STATES AND CANADA, no landscape plant is more commonly used or evokes more nostalgia than the common lilac (*Syringa vulgaris*). For me, lilac bloom is a reminder of Memorial Day observations during my childhood in northern Vermont. No doubt the deliciously fragrant violet and white flowers prompt pleasant memories for most people who have grown up in the North Country, and for that reason we will continue to plant lilacs in spite of their shortcomings.

This is not intended to be a tirade against a plant that's a favorite of just about everyone, but in selecting landscape plants it is useful to maintain perspective by considering each plant's limitations as well as its attractions. And lilacs certainly have limitations.

Although lilacs flower handsomely for one or two weeks (in May or early June in the North), for fifty weeks of the year they are *not* flowering, and not offering much other landscape interest, either. You might gladly tolerate that in return for the fragrant blossoms, but consider limiting the number of lilacs on your property so you can also plant other shrubs with more seasonal variety.

A second disadvantage is that most lilacs grow too large to be used next to one-story buildings, and their only other primary function is to serve as screens. They are tall enough for that, but many do not remain full enough at the base to be really effective without annual pruning. When most of the root suckers are removed annually, as is usually recommended, the remaining plant appears leggy, and it takes skillful pruning to make it fill out. It is easier to allow many root suckers to

Lilacs

remain and fill in the base of the plant, but that may detract from the effectiveness of the plant in bloom.

In some climates, especially in sites with poor air circulation, lilac foliage is almost annually infected with mildew fungus, showing up as gray-white patches on the otherwise deep green foliage. Mildew does little permanent damage other than weakening the plant, but it disfigures the leaves and causes them to fall prematurely. This problem is usually not so severe in the northernmost states and Canada as it is farther south, where late summers are more humid.

Lilacs have been planted in North American gardens since Colonial times, and they were cultivated in Europe centuries earlier. Around the beginning of the present century, a great interest in improved cultivars developed, primarily because of the work of a French nurseryman, Victor Lemoine. A large group of new cultivars, usually called the French hybrids, resulted. Most of those are selections of common lilac, not true hybrids involving two or more species. Of the 500 or more kinds of lilacs that can be found in arboretum collections, most belong to the French hybrid group. They come in shades of white, pink, violet, and blue, with both single and double flowers, and in a range of sizes and growth rates. Most have larger flowers and flower clusters than the old species type, but few are more effective as landscape plants. Ordinarily, the choice of cultivars in any given locality is relatively limited, and you should see them in flower before making a selection, if possible.

Even though most French hybrid lilacs are not hybrids at all, true hybrids do exist. One of these, the so-called Chinese lilac (*Syringa* x *chinensis*), is so common and so functional that it deserves to be singled out. This showy shrub combines the heavy flowering of its common lilac (*S. vulgaris*) parent with some of the gracefulness and fine texture of its cutleaf lilac (*S. laciniata*) parent. The result is a dense shrub that is useful as a visual screen or informal hedge.

As sometimes happens with hybrid groups, there is some confusion about the name of this plant. First of all, the accepted name of Chinese lilac suggests a plant native to China. That is confusing, because hybrids have no native habitat, but are produced through cultivation. The Chinese lilac's cutleaf parent *is* from China, however. Complicating matters, Chinese lilac is often mistakenly called Persian lilac, the correct name for another plant (*S.* x *persica*), which is not native to Persia but is a hybrid between cutleaf lilac and Afghan lilac (*S. afghanica*). Afghan lilac grows wild in Afghanistan and possibly also in Persia, which is now Iran.

Enough for nomenclatural confusion. The point is that plants purchased as Persian lilac more often than not turn out to be Chinese lilac instead, while plants sold as Chinese lilac are usually correctly labeled.

Chinese lilac grows to be almost as tall as common lilac—12 to 16 feet in time. Its leaves are smaller than those of common lilac, but they

form a denser mass, making a superior visual screen. Leaves and flowers are borne lower on Chinese lilac, keeping the plant relatively full at the base. Sometimes it will function as a screen for five to ten years before any pruning becomes necessary.

Flowers of Chinese lilac range from white and pale lavender to rosy purple, and they open at the same time as those of common lilac. The flowers are borne in rather loose panicles, sometimes larger than those of common lilac, but not so deliciously scented. Only a few cultivars are available. The white form 'Alba' is not widely seen. The most common cultivar, variously called 'Red Rothomagensis,' 'Rubra,' and 'Saugeana'—probably all names for the same clone—is extremely vigorous and adaptable, with showy red-purple flowers.

The two related lilacs mentioned earlier are also of landscape interest. Persian lilac is occasionally available and is different enough from Chinese lilac that the two are not interchangeable in landscape use. Persian lilac has smaller leaves and finer texture than Chinese lilac. It seldom grows much taller than 6 feet and is loose and airy in habit, a delightfully graceful plant, but practically useless for screening. The cutleaf lilac has the finest texture of all lilacs, with finely divided small leaves, but otherwise is very similar to Persian lilac. Cold-hardiness of Persian and cutleaf lilac is not well known, since they have not been tested thoroughly in cold climates, but tests in southern Manitoba show that at least some clones of Persian lilac may be about as hardy as Chinese lilac, which will withstand temperatures of −30°F or lower. Cutleaf lilac may be more tender, but is hardy to −20°F or lower.

For best flowering, all lilacs need full sun and reasonably well-drained soil that is not prone to severe drought. If they are allowed to set seeds they may not flower fully the next year. Seed-set in early summer coincides with the beginning of microscopic flower buds, which develop into blossoms that will open the following spring. When there is not enough energy for both processes, seed setting takes precedence. For full flowering annually, spent flower clusters should be cut off as soon as they lose their color. Since double-flowered lilacs are generally sterile, forming neither fruits nor seeds, they usually flower well every year without cutting. The same is true of Chinese lilac, which usually does not form fruits, either.

Lilacs are not trouble free. Blight and wilt diseases, although less common than mildew, are sometimes serious enough to destroy plants if corrective measures are not taken. Borers and scale insects can also destroy plants in time, and leaf miners can disfigure foliage as much as mildew.

Obviously, there are potential costs associated with growing lilacs, in addition to the cost of the original planting. But that is not likely to discourage anyone who is anticipating the spring bloom of lilac's colorful and distinctively fragrant flowers.

The Oleasters

THE OLEASTER FAMILY (Elaeagnaceae) has no monopoly on hardiness, but some of its members show a rare combination of tolerances, thriving in spite of cold, drought, and infertile soil. A few are outstanding landscape plants as well.

Oleasters can be recognized easily by the silver or brown, nearly microscopic scales that cover much of the surface of leaves and stems giving the foliage a silvery or rusty sheen. Their fragrant flowers are not showy, but the single-seeded fruits that follow are conspicuous and sometimes colorful. They are borne freely on all plants of some species, but others are dioecious, with only pistillate (female) or staminate (male) flowers on a single plant.

Oleasters are well suited to dry soils and are unusually tolerant of seaside and roadside salt. Like alders, bayberry, and many legumes, they are able to use atmospheric nitrogen with the help of nitrogen-fixing bacteria that inhabit nodules on their roots. Consequently, they can thrive in soils that are low in nitrogen, just as alfalfa and clover do.

The best known oleaster is probably Russian olive (*Elaeagnus angustifolia*), an import from central Asia and southern Europe. This huge shrub or small tree (depending on how it is trained) can grow to 20 feet or more in height, with an almost equal spread. Its foliage emerges silvery-white, creating a striking effect in late spring to midsummer, heightened by the small but fragrant, pale yellow flowers which open in early summer. The silvery color fades as summer wears on, but never completely disappears until leaf-fall in early autumn. Greenish-yellow fruits resembling small olives, but flecked with silvery scales, add interest in late summer and early autumn.

Russian olive, once recommended enthusiastically for wildlife cover, windbreaks, and other large-scale plantings, has fallen into disfavor in

86

some areas because of its susceptibility to trunk canker and wilt diseases. But it is still useful in areas where those diseases are not prevalent, and it will grow in cold climates, withstanding temperatures of −40°F and lower.

Perhaps the most useful member of the oleaster family is autumn olive (*Elaeagnus umbellata*), a shrub from the Far East that grows 10 to 12 feet tall. In late spring it bears large quantities of fragrant, pale yellow flowers, which develop into silverflecked red fruits in early autumn. Recommended by the U.S. Soil Conservation Service for wildlife planting, this shrub makes an excellent visual screen as well, as its lightly silvered green foliage makes a dense mass with little or no pruning. It is less troublesome than Russian olive, is equally adapted to poor, dry soils, and is cold-hardy where annual minimum temperatures average −20°F to −25°F.

Another hardy member of the oleaster family, native to the northern Great Plains and useful where winter minimum temperatures average −40°F and lower, is buffalo-berry (*Shepherdia argentea*). This shrub, growing to 15 or 20 feet tall, strongly resembles Russian olive, with its narrow, silvered leaves and open growth habit, but it can be distinguished from all *Elaeagnus* species by its opposite leaf arrangement. Another difference is that buffalo-berry is dioecious. Only pistillate (female) plants bear the scarlet fruits, which add considerable interest in late summer and are valued for making preserves where the plant grows wild. As with most other dioecious species, an occasional male plant should be included in plantings for pollination.

Still another member of this family is the distinctive sea buckthorn (*Hippophaë rhamnoides*), imported from north-central Asia and cold-hardy to at least −40°F. Like *Shepherdia*, it is dioecious; pistillate plants bear large numbers of small, orange-yellow fruits, tightly clustered close to the stems. Ripening in late summer, they hold their color through autumn and well into winter in mild climates. Leaves are about two inches long and very narrow, giving the plant an open, twiggy appearance and allowing the fruits to show clearly.

Sea buckthorn is much too sparse in habit to be useful as a screen, but it is effective in situations where its foliage and fruit provide needed accent in summer. This shrub has only one bad feature: once established, it spreads by root suckers. That may not be a serious problem in mass plantings, but it can be troublesome in a confined setting. One solution is to cut off all unwanted suckers annually. Another is to let suckers grow right up to the edge of a lawn, where regular mowing will control them.

All of these members of the oleaster family have distinctively silvered summer foliage and interesting fruit. Where summer color is desired and tolerance of drought, salt, and cold winters are important, they are well worth considering.

Pagoda
Dogwood

OF THE DOGWOODS THAT ARE TREES rather than shrubs, the pagoda dogwood (*Cornus alternifolia*) is the only one that is hardy in areas where winter temperatures regularly fall below −20°F. While not as magnificent as the less hardy flowering dogwood (*Cornus florida*), it does have some similarities, as well as other good features distinctly its own.

While it is sometimes shrubby in the wild, the pagoda dogwood can function well in landscape use as a small tree, growing 15 to 20 feet tall, usually with multiple trunks. Its most striking feature is its strongly tiered branching, suggesting a Japanese pagoda—hence its common name. This layered form is most apparent when accentuated by the creamy white flowers, individually small but borne in flat clusters 2 inches or more across and close enough together to form almost continuous layers of bloom in late spring.

As the flowers drop, small green fruits can be seen forming in the clusters. By July they are pea-size, and a month later they ripen to a dark, inky blue and are displayed on bright red stalks, accentuating the layered branching just as the flowers did earlier, until they are taken by birds in early autumn. After the foliage turns dull reddish purple and falls in midautumn, the plant remains quietly interesting through the winter, so strikingly do the bare green branches and twigs continue to outline the horizontal branching pattern.

In spite of the Japanese implications of its name, pagoda dogwood is native to eastern North America, from New Brunswick to Minnesota and southward in the Appalachian Mountains to Georgia and Alabama. Its distinctive leaves, with veins curving and running parallel to the leaf margins, mark it as a dogwood, and it can just as easily be recognized as pagoda dogwood by its alternate leaves. The only other dogwood with alternate leaves that is ever planted in the Northeast is the giant dogwood (*Cornus controversa*), a rarely cultivated Asian tree.

Like flowering dogwood, pagoda dogwood grows best in reasonably moist, well-drained soil that is at least slightly acidic. Its hardiness to cold makes it a logical choice to stand in for flowering dogwood in northern climates.

Transplanting sometimes has proved difficult, usually because inexperienced landscapers have tried to move trees directly from the wild to landscape sites. Wild trees have rangy roots, which are often cut off when the tree is dug up. Because of this root damage, attempts at direct transplanting of wild trees usually are doomed to failure. Success is more likely if you start with trees that have been nursery-grown, or at least transplanted in a nursery for a year or two if they were originally taken from the wild. These previously transplanted trees will have had a chance to develop compact root systems, which are more adaptable to transplanting when they are moved again.

Transplanting time for most trees in northern areas is spring, but many trees can be moved much later by professionals. Young trees grown in containers can be transplanted during most of the summer in northern areas, if the ground is then mulched before winter sets in, to prevent frost heaving. In mild climates, autumn transplanting may even be preferred. In areas where mice and rabbits are known to be a problem, remember to protect young tree trunks with wire screening.

The choice of trees should be governed by their usefulness as well as their beauty, and pagoda dogwood is functional as well as attractive. As a patio tree it should be planted about 6 to 8 feet from the paved sitting area. As it grows, prune away a lower branch or two each year, gradually raising the foliage canopy on the trunk so that it offers an overhead enclosure without encroaching on your sitting space.

When using pagoda dogwood as a lawn specimen or in a shrub planting, allow the lower branches to remain, all the way to the ground, but do not try to grow grass underneath or you will create a serious maintenance problem. Remove the existing turf instead, and substitute a neutral-colored mulch such as wood chips or bark, so you won't have to maneuver a lawnmower under tree branches.

Pagoda dogwood also can be used to soften the strong vertical line of a building corner or entrance. Plant about 6 feet from the building, or even farther away if the roof has an overhang that will interfere with rainfall, or if the building is two or more stories in height. When used in any of these ways, pagoda dogwood will be an asset both functionally and aesthetically.

Serviceberries

THE SERVICEBERRIES ARE UNOBTRUSIVE PLANTS that fit easily into the natural or naturalized landscape. Yet they are colorful enough for accent, with billowy white bloom in early spring and scarlet-orange foliage in autumn, and their shapely trunks with silvery gray bark are effective throughout the year. Some are low, thicket-forming shrubs. Others are large enough to serve as small shade trees. Most are equally at home in well-drained or moist, even swampy, soil.

Knowing serviceberries by their correct names is a challenge to amateurs and professionals alike. They have been known by many names at different times and in different places: from the sarvistree of Colonial days, to shadblow, shadbush, juneberry, serviceberry, the *petite poires* of French-speaking Quebec, and the saskatoon of the Canadian prairies. Once we agree that any of these names refers to some member of the genus *Amelanchier*, we are faced with long-standing disputes about the correct splitting of that genus into individual species, and about the correct name for each. Add to this the tendency of species to interbreed, and it is easy to see why there is confusion. These problems are confusing to the professional plantsman, but happily they can usually be ignored by the layman. Since only a few serviceberries are available in nurseries, only these few need be considered for landscape use. And people wishing to transplant other native species of serviceberry from the wild can do so without knowing their specific names, since all of the natives are worthy landscape plants.

When using serviceberries, it is helpful to recognize that they fall into two groups: the relatively low types that spread by underground runners into thickets, and the taller, more treelike types. The most

90

common thicket-forming species are dwarf serviceberry (*Amelanchier spicata*), low serviceberry (*A. humilis*), running serviceberry (*A. stolonifera*), and thicket serviceberry (*A. oblongifolia*). These can be planted in masses, or in a mixed border, or they can be naturalized. They are widely adaptable either to dry, rocky soil, or to the moist soils of stream banks. Seldom will more than one of these species be available at a nursery, but they are so similar that it matters little which is used.

Tree serviceberries most often obtainable for planting include two natives of the Northeast and hybrids between them. The shadblow, or downy serviceberry (*Amelanchier arborea*), often still called *A. canadensis*, is the largest of all, occasionally reaching heights of 60 feet in the South, but in landscape use a small tree up to 30 feet tall. The young foliage, finely coated with silky hairs, emerges a misty, silvery green color in early spring, quickly giving way to white as the flowers open, and just as quickly returning to silvery green as petals fall. The leaves lose most of their downy appearance as they mature, and turn medium green, providing a neutral background for the edible dull red to purple fruits, which are quickly taken by birds as they ripen in midsummer.

The longest-lasting seasonal display comes in autumn, when the foliage turns to russet-gold or red-orange, depending on the weather in a particular year. When the foliage has finally fallen, the single- or multiple-trunked framework and silvery gray bark keep the tree interesting all winter.

The other native, Allegheny serviceberry (*Amelanchier laevis*), is similar to shadblow serviceberry in landscape character. But there are subtle differences between the two. Allegheny serviceberry is not quite as large a tree, and it reputedly does not grow as well in wet soils. Its new foliage is not downy, but distinctly red at emergence, contrasting with the white flowers that quickly follow. By fruiting time, there is little apparent difference between the two, except that the fruits of Allegheny serviceberry are more juicy and sweet than those of downy serviceberry. In fact, they are sometimes used for pies and preserves by humans alert and agile enough to harvest them before they are discovered by birds.

The third tree type, apple serviceberry (*Amelanchier* x *grandiflora*), is actually a hybrid between the two native tree serviceberries. Not surprisingly, it is intermediate between the parents except in having larger flowers and fruits than either. There is a variety with pink-tinged flowers, seldom available commercially and inclined to fade quickly to white.

When all is considered, the tree serviceberries are so similar that one would need compelling reasons to insist on one over another in most landscape situations. Whichever one is selected or accepted, it will prove a reliable small tree, with varied and quickly changing landscape moods, and character at all seasons.

Sumacs

SUMACS (*Rhus* species) are common roadside shrubs in the north-eastern and north-central United States. They are so common, in fact, that we often overlook them as landscape plants. Yet they serve two important functions in natural and constructed landscapes: they provide large-scale mass in highway settings, and their coarse texture can contribute a special accent to smaller-scale landscapes.

Four tall-growing sumacs are native to eastern North America. One of these, poison sumac (*Rhus vernix*), a native of swamps in much of the eastern half of the country, obviously should be shunned rather than planted. The other three, shining sumac (*R. copallina*), smooth sumac (*R. glabra*), and staghorn sumac (*R. typhina*), are more widespread within the same area and are useful and handsome additions to many landscapes.

Staghorn sumac grows wild from the northeastern United States and adjacent Canada southward to Georgia and westward to Iowa. Shining sumac extends farther, to Minnesota and Texas. Smooth sumac is the most widely distributed of all, reaching westward to British Columbia. All three are found on well-drained to dry soils, usually in full sun. Throughout their ranges, they invade roadsides and other areas where soil and vegetation have been disturbed.

Sumacs often form large thickets, giving the impression of great mass during the leafy season. If they were not so commonplace, they might be thought to have a tropical look. Their compound leaves, which can be as long as 2 feet or more, give a distinctively coarse appearance. Smooth sumac grows as tall as 15 feet, while staghorn sumac and shining sumac occasionally attain almost twice that height.

The greenish yellow flowers, in erect clusters 6 to 8 inches long, add minor interest in summer but are hardly showy. Since sumacs are dioecious, flowers of only one sex are found on an individual plant, or in an entire thicket formed by suckering from an individual plant. That becomes more important later, as only pistillate (female) plants bear fruit. The fuzzy fruits are borne in more-or-less clublike clusters, about 6 inches long, adding color to the landscape from late summer or early autumn until midwinter.

As interesting as sumacs are in summer, they become absolutely spectacular in autumn as their foliage turns deep red and then bright scarlet before falling. After leaf-drop, the fruiting clusters on pistillate plants continue to add color.

Staghorn sumac has still another element of interest. The fuzzy terminal branches of staminate (male) plants, where flowers were borne earlier, look somewhat like velvety antlers in winter and give the shrub its common name.

Sumacs are always at their best in sunny sites, but will tolerate light shade. They grow well in a wide range of soils, from dry and sandy to fairly moist and heavy, but they are not good choices for wet soils. As their native ranges suggest, they are widely adaptable to climate, but that does not mean all plants are adaptable to all climates within their native areas. In fact, plants originating in the Deep South probably will not survive northern winters. As with other wide-ranging trees and shrubs, it is usually a good idea to use plants of local origin.

Shining sumac grows wild where minimum winter temperatures average −20°F or lower; staghorn sumac is found where temperatures drop 10 degrees lower than that, and smooth sumac grows in places that are slightly colder yet. Shining sumac may not be fully hardy in the coldest parts of the Northeast, nor in northern Minnesota, but the other two sumacs perform well in those areas.

Two cut-leaved sumacs are especially useful in architectonic settings —those where buildings and pavement predominate, creating a formal impression that can be effectively complemented by a few plants (or even a single plant) with striking texture or pattern. Cut-leaved staghorn sumac (*Rhus typhina* 'Dissecta') is the more common of the two, with finely dissected foliage which turns bright orange in autumn, irregularly crooked branches, and the fruits and twigs typical of staghorn sumac in winter. Cut-leaved smooth sumac (*R. glabra* 'Laciniata') has similar foliage but may be more difficult to find in nurseries.

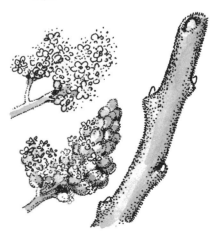

In fact, sumacs generally are not easy to locate in nurseries, but at least a few do offer them for sale. Transplanting from wild stands, a waste of time with many plants, works reasonably well with sumacs. It is best done when the leaves are falling in autumn, or in early spring. Dig out small shoots with as many fibrous roots as possible and replant them in an extra flower bed where they can be watered-in thoroughly. A year later, they can be transplanted in the same way to a permanent location. Once established, small plants will grow quickly, developing into a mass of shrubbery and providing landscape interest through much of the year.

93

Wayfaring Tree

SELECTING LANDSCAPE PLANTS CAN BE DISCOURAGING for residents of the coldest parts of the United States, but prospects are sometimes better than they seem. There is an impressive list of truly hardy shrubs and trees for such rigorous climates as those of northern New England and the northern Great Lakes region. One of the most useful of these is wayfaring tree (*Viburnum lantana*), a Eurasian plant that is so well adapted to our region that it has escaped cultivation and now grows wild in a few localities. It may be this tendency, and its appearance along roadsides in the wild, that has given the plant its common name of wayfaring tree.

Wayfaring tree, like most viburnums, is a functional plant with quiet seasonal interest during most of the year. Little-noticed while leafless in winter, it becomes conspicuous in midspring when leaves and flat clusters of small, creamy white flowers emerge together. After the flowers fall, the leaves continue to expand, becoming 4 to 5 inches long and almost as wide, with their deeply impressed veins giving a wrinkled or corrugated appearance. By midsummer, growth has stopped and the foliage becomes leathery and dark green, as it will remain until autumn, when it falls with little change of color.

Flattened fruits begin to form in early summer, in the same flat clusters that bore flowers earlier. By late summer, they begin to change color—from pale green through yellow to red, then suddenly to blue-black at maturity. Individual fruits change color at different times; it is not unusual to see yellow-green, red, and blue-black fruits all in the same cluster, displayed effectively against the dark green foliage. When fully ripe, they shrivel and look like small raisins. At this stage they may be taken immediately by birds, or left hanging until winter, when more desirable fruits have been eaten or lie on the ground under snow cover.

Functionally, wayfaring tree is useful for visual screening. It attains a height of 8 to 10 feet after a few years of strong growth, and eventually grows 12 to 15 feet tall. Its strong upright development comes at the expense of lateral spread at first, sometimes leaving the lower part of the plant leggy and sparse. "Facing" shrubs, planted 3 or 4 feet from the larger ones to make the lower part of the screen more dense, are sometimes needed. In fact, wayfaring tree is often best used in combination with other shrubs for variety in seasonal effects. It is also valued for planting near the corners of two-story homes or other buildings to provide a transition between building and ground lines.

Wayfaring tree is among the most drought-resistant of all viburnums, and grows well in the driest garden soils of the Northeast. It does best in well-drained soil, but will tolerate occasional wetness. Although it performs reasonably well in considerable, but not full, shade, for heavy flowering and fruiting it should receive as much sun as possible.

Wayfaring tree has been abandoned by a few nurseries in favor of more showy but less hardy varieties. Yet many northern nurseries still carry this functional plant and it should not be difficult to locate. Fortunately, it has few troubles that require spraying or other maintenance. The tendency of this Eurasian shrub to make itself at home in our areas may lead it to become a minor weed in some situations, but the same faculty also guarantees its adaptability and makes it one of the most useful shrubs for the Northeast's coldest climates.

95

Witch Hazel

COMMON WITCH HAZEL (*Hamamelis virginiana*) is surely one of the most interesting native shrubs of eastern North America. Its history of medicinal use began long before the coming of Europeans to this continent, it has traditionally been the preferred "water witch" of dowsers, and its flowers and foliage add bright color to the autumn woodlands. In addition to all this it is a useful landscape plant.

Legend has it that the appearance of small, spidery, yellow flowers after leaf-fall in autumn caught the interest of American Indians and led them to use the plant for healing. Its modern-day medicinal use goes back more than a century, to the time when the Dickinson family of Connecticut started to produce a distilled extract that can still be obtained today. The custom of using forked sticks of witch hazel for dowsing—locating underground water—has long been practiced by country folk, and the woodland charm of this shrub is well-appreciated by outdoor enthusiasts. But landscape use of witch hazel is not so familiar to most people.

Even though it grows in the woods as an understory shrub, often in rather deep shade, witch hazel does equally well in the open, where it assumes a more compact shape but retains its strongly horizontal branching. Within a few years it grows 8 to 10 feet tall, eventually reaching at least 15 feet in height and nearly twice that in spread, if there is enough space for it to develop fully. It can function as a screen,

96

but is not often used for that purpose because it is not quite full enough as a young shrub and grows so large at maturity that it may exceed the available space. Perhaps the most effective use of witch hazel is along borders of woodlands, where enough light is available to promote heavy flowering and the flowers are highlighted against the dark background of the woods. This shrub is also effective when planted where people will walk by it frequently in autumn, perhaps by an entry walk or drive, or outside large windows where its autumn show can be seen at close range from inside as well as outside.

Since witch hazel becomes very large, pruning may be necessary, either to restrict its size or, if desired, to train it into a small, multiple-stemmed patio tree. Other than this, it needs little or no maintenance, for it has no serious problems.

Common witch hazel grows wild in areas of the Northeast where winter temperatures regularly reach $-15°F$ to $-20°F$, with occasional dips to $-25°F$ to $-30°F$, and this probably represents the climatic extremes for landscape use as well. This shrub can be planted either in full sun or shade, but flowering will be heavier and slightly earlier in full sun. Since transplanting can be tricky, it's best to buy container-grown shrubs from a nursery. They should thrive in any good, well-drained soil.

Leaves of witch hazel are shallowly lobed and medium green, forming a clean-looking, irregular foliage mass. In autumn they turn clear golden yellow, before or during flowering. The spicily fragrant, bright yellow flowers extend the seasonal color, sometimes for as long as three weeks after the leaves have fallen. Individual plants vary by at least a month in flowering time. Selections for superior flowering evidently have not been made, but could be. The ideal plant might well be one with early and reliable fall foliage color followed by flowering after the foliage has fallen and no longer obscures the effect. Such plants can be found in rows of seedlings in nurseries and could be propagated by cuttings, retaining their character.

Other than in autumn, witch hazel shows little landscape color, but the fruiting capsules are interesting at close range. They are dull green in summer and turn brown as they dry in autumn. During this drying process, stresses build up in the hard capsule walls until they break open at the seams. This happens explosively, discharging the small, shiny black seeds for some distance. I have heard of hikers pocketing a few capsules, emptying them onto a bedside stand in the evening, and being awakened by the discharges during the night.

Witch hazel will enhance any landscape with its quiet but distinctive autumnal flowering and its neutral but pleasing foliage that turns bright yellow in fall. Add freedom from maintenance to those attributes, and the result is a shrub that deserves wider consideration for landscape use.

97

98

DECIDUOUS MEDIUM TREES (24 to 48 feet tall) VII

TREES THAT CAN BE COUNTED ON to remain below about 50 feet in height are large enough for many landscape situations. Caring for such trees is much less costly than for large trees, and so is removal, when necessary.

Before planting trees, carefully consider how large they need to be for the intended function—and how large they are likely to become. Sometimes a really large tree is the appropriate choice, but sometimes it is not. Knowing which size is appropriate will repay the time and effort invested in finding out.

The medium trees listed are among the best for cold climates, but consider others, such as striped maple (*Acer pensylvanicum*), yellow and sweet birch (*Betula alleghaniensis* and *B. lenta*), aspens (*Populus grandidentata* and *P. tremuloides*), and Mongolian linden (*Tilia mongolica*).

American Hornbeam

PICTURE A GARDEN TREE with smooth, sinewy, gray trunk and branches, delicate foliage and interesting fruits in summer, and a brilliant display of red-orange foliage in autumn. Add to this enough hardiness to make the tree useful in all of New England and comparable climates in the Midwest—and you have the American hornbeam (*Carpinus caroliniana*), a rugged native of our forests and one of the finest landscape trees.

Residents of the North Country are often discouraged by the failure of plants they have admired in gardens farther south, and the idea has spread that few plants are hardy enough to grow in northern areas. American hornbeam is an outstanding example of a tree handsome and useful enough to grace any landscape, hardy enough to grow anywhere in our area.

Like many other trees, *Carpinus caroliniana* goes under different local names. In Vermont, for instance, it is known as blue beech, and in early Colonial days its branches were the instrument used by the Green Mountain Boys to administer the "beech seal" to the backs of New Yorkers involved in land-grant disputes. In other areas, this tree and its related species, the hop-hornbeam (*Ostrya virginiana*), are alternately called ironwood.

When planted in a man-made landscape, with plenty of room in which to grow, American hornbeam will become a handsome, rounded shade tree, with an interesting branching framework that gives it character even in winter. With its muscled trunk and branches, delicate foliage and pendulous fruiting clusters, and autumn foliage color, it is truly a four-season tree. Yet none of its color and accent are so strong as to make it seem out of place in a natural landscape.

Generally speaking, landscape trees range from the fast-growing, soft-wooded kind that are often prone to storm breakage and disease to the slow-growing, durable varieties that age gracefully and bridge human generations. American hornbeam falls toward the slow-growing end of this spectrum, reaching a height of 10 to 15 feet (and similar spread) ten years after planting as a 6-foot sapling. But remember that proper planting and good cultural practices (annual fertilization and an occasional soaking during dry weather) can result in much faster growth than average, even for slow-growing trees such as American hornbeam. Details on cultural methods can be obtained from cooperative extension service offices.

This tree is widely adaptable, as shown by its natural distribution, from Nova Scotia to Minnesota and Florida to Texas. It will grow in virtually any well-drained soil over a wide range of soil acidity and fertility. But it is not a good choice for wet, poorly drained sites. A word of caution: with American hornbeam as well as many other species, use stock of northern origin for planting in northern areas.

American hornbeam has been described as difficult to transplant, and it does require a little more care in transplanting than many other trees. But with care in digging and handling during moving, it can be transplanted very successfully. Container-grown trees, which do not experience root loss in moving, can be transplanted even more easily. Trees dug from nursery rows should be transplanted as early as possible in spring, before buds expand, but container-grown trees can be planted any time from then until midsummer, still leaving time for establishment before the onset of winter. Native trees can be transplanted from the woods into landscape situations, but this is a tricky operation at best, and should be left to the commercial nurseryman.

A common complaint about landscape plants is: "I have been told that _____ is an excellent tree to use, but I can't find it in my local nursery." This has been said more than once about American hornbeam. Most nurseries carry plants they know they can sell quickly. Relatively few are "missionaries," trying to educate their clients about better quality plants. Consequently, trees like American hornbeam, of high quality but not "best-sellers," are not offered for sale by every nursery. Fortunately, a scattering of nurseries in the Northeast *do* carry this tree, and still others will custom-order trees from wholesale nurseries for future delivery.

North Country residents looking for a modest-size landscape tree that will reflect the seasonality and character of the area they live in will do well to consider this handsome native tree.

American Yellowwood

ONE OF THE MOST COLORFUL FLOWERING TREES that can be grown in cold climates is American yellowwood (*Cladrastis lutea*). This handsome native of the southeastern United States has been grown in cultivation since the early nineteenth century, and it still has much to offer today.

Yellowwood grows wild in Kentucky, Tennessee, and North Carolina, and in a few spots in Ohio, Indiana, and Missouri, reaching heights of 40 to 50 feet. It is found primarily in well-drained, fertile soils, but will also grow in dry soils, once well established, over a broad range of soil acidity and even in neutral or slightly alkaline soils.

A member of the Legume family (Leguminosae), yellowwood has fragrant white, pea-size flowers, individually about an inch across and borne in hanging clusters 10 to 15 inches long, resembling white wisteria flowers. These reach full bloom in June in the North. Trees bear only a partial crop of flowers in some years, but about every second or third year are covered with great numbers of flower clusters, making a spectacle that must have delighted early settlers in the southern Appalachians when they first saw them. The compound leaves begin to unfold at flowering time, then quickly expand to form a dense, dark green canopy for the rest of summer. In autumn, foliage turns delicate orange or yellow before falling. The small fruits add little landscape interest.

This tree has silvery gray bark similar to that of American beech. But in shape it is decidedly different from beech. The flowing lines of the main limbs as they branch off have a sculpted look and when darkened by rain they give the effect of weathered bronze.

A problem sometimes arises from the narrow branching angles that produce this characteristic flowing look. The narrow crotches that result may form tight pockets where water can collect, encouraging decay. Main branches of older trees occasionally decline and then die from problems associated with the narrow crotch. Because of this it is a good idea to have trees checked by an arborist if they show weak growth on one side, so that the problem can be corrected early.

Yellowwood can be used as a landscape tree far north of its native range. It is cold-hardy where annual minimum temperatures average −20°F to −25°F and sometimes fall to −30°F. This makes it useful in southern New England, the milder half of northern New England, all but the very coldest parts of upstate New York, Michigan's lower peninsula, the southern half of Wisconsin, and southern Minnesota.

Pruning of yellowwood offers a special problem because this tree has an extremely heavy sap flow in spring, at the time when other trees are often pruned. To avoid damage it is important to prune such trees in summer rather than spring. Perhaps even more to the point, it is seldom necessary to prune this tree at all, except when the early branching framework is being developed or to remove damaged or rubbing branches.

Transplanting is tricky enough to be best left to professionals in most cases. Spring is the best time to do it in the North, but it should be done without simultaneous top pruning, because of the heavy sap flow.

Chances of success in transplanting can be improved greatly by root pruning. This means digging vertically in a circle around the tree to sever roots in the same way that would be done in digging the root ball for transplanting. The difference is that the root ball is not removed until months later, after many new roots have formed within the root ball. For spring transplanting, root prune in late summer or early autumn and fertilize and water thoroughly, if necessary, at the same time. New roots will form rapidly if there is adequate moisture and many more active roots can be moved in spring than would have been present in the soil ball without root pruning.

Root pruning, by the way, is useful as preparation for transplanting many other kinds of trees. It is hard work and requires advance planning, but it usually pays off handsomely in faster establishment in the new site, or sometimes in success rather than failure.

A selection of yellowwood with light pink flowers, 'Rosea,' is just becoming commercially available. At least one nursery, perhaps others, now offer it for sale, but it is not likely to be widely available for some time.

Meanwhile, the white-flowering form is growing in popularity and is being used more widely than ever before. As a small to medium-size shade tree, interesting in all seasons, it is a truly beautiful and useful landscape plant.

Amur Corktree

SOME OF THE MOST VALUABLE LANDSCAPE PLANTS for the colder climates of North America have originated in the Amur River region of Manchuria and Siberia. One of these is the Amur corktree (*Phellodendron amurense*), a wide-spreading tree with massive, picturesque limbs and deeply furrowed, corky bark.

Along with many tropicals and a few temperate-zone trees and shrubs, Amur corktree belongs to the Rue family (Rutaceae). Members of this family contain aromatic oils that can be released by rubbing or crushing. The most familiar example is the rind of citrus fruits. Leaves and fruits of Amur corktree are also aromatic, but the oil released by crushing smells more like turpentine than citrus oil.

Amur corktree is an effective lawn or patio shade tree, but is less useful as a street tree because of the lateral spread of its canopy. The related Sakhalin corktree (*P. sachalinense*) grows more upright, yet is too large for most urban sites. The Chinese corktree (*P. chinense*) is smaller but less winter-hardy and is seldom available commercially.

The massive limbs of Amur corktree spread widely from a short trunk, so that at maturity the tree is at least as wide as it is tall. When in leaf, the tree's canopy serves as a lacy umbrella that casts a mottled shade, making it a pleasant tree to relax under. The dark green foliage is unusually free of insects and diseases, and in some years turns pale yellow before falling in autumn. Then almost all the leaves may fall in a single night, leaving the branches suddenly and dramatically exposed.

From then until spring the massive limbs and corky, corrugated bark give the tree a dominant place in the winter landscape.

Flowers of both male and female trees (sexes are separate in all the corktrees) are inconspicuous, but clusters of green, pea-size fruits appear on female trees in late summer, turn black as they ripen in autumn, and are a minor litter problem when they drop.

In temperate-zone trees the first evidence of preparation for winter is the cessation of stem growth in summer in response to shortening days. Many trees and shrubs do this by forming terminal buds that remain dormant until the following spring, when they give rise to the new year's growth. Others, such as common lilac, redbud, and Amur corktree, do not form terminal buds. Instead, their stem tips simply separate from the plant and fall off, leaving a small scar just above the uppermost lateral bud of each stem. This lateral bud then takes over the role of a terminal bud, sending forth new stem growth the following spring. Since stem tips of Amur corktree drop off long before autumn, the process will be unnoticed by any but the most careful observer. The precise time when this happens will vary somewhat from tree to tree. Those that drop their stem tips earliest can be expected to begin the process of cold acclimation earliest, and are best adapted to withstand the first severe cold of autumn in rigorous climates.

We might expect that this Manchurian tree would be adaptable to the coldest climates of the United States, since this is generally true for other trees from the same region. But vigorous young corktrees growing in fertile soil occasionally are damaged by cold during the first two or three winters after transplanting. The vigor of such trees delays acclimation to the cold in autumn, but several precautions can be taken to avoid or minimize the problem:

(1) Select trees that have been growing for a year or two in a local nursery, if possible. Individual trees vary in hardiness, and a local trial may eliminate the least hardy individuals before you buy them.

(2) Don't plant in "frost-pockets." Such sites, located in topographic depressions where cold air can settle, are especially prone to late spring and early fall freezes.

(3) Don't fertilize the tree until at least a year or two after planting, and then fertilize only in late autumn, when temperatures are low enough to prevent stimulation of late activity, or in early spring.

(4) Prune only in late winter or spring, or not at all. Usually this will not be necessary except to remove any dead wood.

In areas where minimum temperatures seldom fall below −15°F, these precautions are not necessary. In colder areas, they apply equally well to many other trees and shrubs.

Amur corktree is fairly widely available in nurseries in the northern parts of the country, and it is easily transplanted. Once established, it is a relatively long-lived, trouble-free, and distinctive shade tree.

105

Bird Cherries

BIRD CHERRIES ARE THOSE CHERRIES that bear small flowers and fruits in racemes (elongated clusters). Most members of this group have little value as landscape plants, but four are worth considering in cold climates.

One of the most impressive of this group is the European bird cherry (*Prunus padus*), a tree that grows quickly to heights of 20 to 30 feet, and sometimes taller. It produces thousands of small, fragrant, white flowers, in gracefully drooping to pendulous clusters, sometimes 6 inches long. Flowers open with the rapidly expanding foliage, giving a billowy effect in midspring. The small cherries, only about a quarter inch across, ripen black in midsummer and are taken quickly by birds. For the remainder of the year this tree is not colorful, but it is more trouble free than most of its relatives, and adaptable to climates where annual minimum temperatures average lower than −30°F. Several cultivars have been selected for superior flowering effect. 'Commutata' flowers two to three weeks before the species type, beginning when the leaves have barely started to unfold. 'Plena,' with double flowers, and 'Watereri,' with clusters up to 8 inches long, are superior for flowering interest, but not always available.

The largest member of the bird cherry group, the native black cherry (*Prunus serotina*) of eastern North America, has even smaller flowers than European bird cherry, small fruits ripening black in late summer, and fairly interesting bark. It grows wild from Ontario and North Dakota to northern Florida and Texas, and trees from northern seed sources can withstand the lowest temperatures experienced in the northeastern United States and adjacent Canada. Since this tree becomes large and drops considerable twig and fruit litter, it is best reserved for parklike or naturalized situations. Trees of mature size are seldom seen, as many have been harvested for their wood, which is considered second only to walnut for making fine furniture.

Fruits of black cherry are usually taken promptly by birds as soon as they ripen, but they also can be used for making wines and flavorings for humans. Eaten fresh, they are bitter but not so astringent as those of chokecherry.

Another native of much of eastern North America is the common chokecherry of roadsides (*Prunus virginiana*). This shrub or small, scrubby tree has little landscape interest and is favorite food for tent caterpillars over the eastern part of its range. The only reason for considering it at all is its purple-leaved variant 'Schubert,' which has distinctive landscape interest. Its leaves are larger and smoother than those of the purple-leaved plum, and unlike any other purple-leaved shrub or tree the leaves are pea green as they unfold, then quickly turn purple. While growth is active, the green leaves of the new growing tips are contrasted against the purple foliage mass. 'Schubert' chokecherry is more cold-hardy than any of the purple-leaved plums or even the purple-leaved sand cherry, withstanding winter temperatures of −45°F or lower.

Last but not least is the Amur chokecherry (*Prunus maackii*), a tree about the same size as European bird cherry, from the Amur River region of Manchuria. This tree is a natural for winter interest, with smooth, peeling, amber bark, vaguely reminiscent of that of yellow birch (*Betula alleghaniensis*) or paperbark maple (*Acer griseum*). The winter bark interest continues throughout the year, but flowering and fruiting are no more colorful than that of black cherry and chokecherry. Like 'Schubert' chokecherry, Amur chokecherry is cold-hardy enough to perform well in the most northern areas. In less severe climates, there are probably better choices for bark interest, including some of the more tender cherries and paperbark maple.

Cherries are prone to many disease and pest problems. Mildew and leaf spot diseases can do even greater damage. But the greatest single problem of the bird cherry group, in the Northeast at least, is the eastern tent caterpillar. This pest is so troublesome that wild cherries have been deliberately eradicated from some areas to control it. In areas where tent caterpillars are active (new residents can check with their neighbors), black cherry and chokecherry probably should not be planted at all, but fortunately the Amur chokecherry and bird cherry are less troubled. In any case, it is a good idea to watch any cherry with some vigilance so problems can be spotted early and controlled promptly. When this is done the special effects available from these plants will add significantly to the seasonal interest of any landscape in which they are included.

107

Magnolias

FEW TREES ARE MORE FIRMLY ASSOCIATED with soft southern breezes than magnolias, and it may come as a surprise that some of them are adapted to northern regions with temperatures of −20°F or lower. Only a few, to be sure, but those few offer considerable variety and landscape interest.

Magnolias vary from small, shrubby trees such as star magnolia (*Magnolia stellata*) to large trees such as cucumbertree magnolia (*M. acuminata*). Those hardy in the North are deciduous, and all have silvery gray bark that is especially colorful in winter.

The magnolia most commonly grown in the North is the saucer magnolia (*Magnolia* x *soulangiana*), a hybrid between two Asian species. This deciduous tree, growing to 20 feet or more in height, bears huge pink or purplish flowers, sometimes 6 inches across, in early spring before the leaves unfold. The silvery gray bark of twigs and branches complements the spring flower color and continues to add interest throughout the year. Foliage is medium green, rather coarse in texture, and sweetly aromatic when crushed. Saucer magnolia grows best in soils that are not extremely wet or dry. It tolerates minimum temperatures to −20°F, but the flowers occasionally are nipped by late freezes in spring.

Star magnolia (*M. stellata*), another popular Asian species, is much smaller, remaining below 10 feet in height for many years. In early spring—even earlier than saucer magnolia—it bears large numbers of starlike flowers, each with more than a dozen tepals (petals and petal-like sepals). Flowering begins when plants are quite young, a distinct asset to those of us with little patience. This plant is about as cold-hardy as saucer magnolia, but its earlier flowers are more likely to suffer from spring frost. Because of its small size it usually is used as a specimen rather than a shade or patio tree.

A larger relative of star magnolia is Kobus magnolia (*M. kobus*), a tree growing as large as saucer magnolia. Its white flowers have only half as many tepals as those of star magnolia and are not usually borne in large numbers until the tree is at least twenty years old. This probably is the most cold-hardy of all the Asian magnolias, useful where annual minimum temperatures average −25°F and occasionally fall to −30°F to −35°F.

One of the most impressive of the Asian magnolias is the cultivar 'Merrill,' a hybrid between the Kobus and star magnolias. This tree becomes almost as large as Kobus magnolia, reaching a height of at least 20 feet in time. Its flowers have fewer tepals than those of star magnolia, but are slightly larger and equally showy. Even more important, this hybrid has inherited the precocious flowering of its star magnolia parent, and most of the hardiness of the Kobus magnolia parent.

Not all hardy magnolias are of Asian origin. Two North American species are as cold-hardy as their Asian counterparts, and offer distinctive landscape interest as well.

Cucumbertree magnolia (*M. acuminata*), native from New York to Georgia and Arkansas, becomes a huge tree, sometimes to 100 feet tall, with massive trunk and branches and a dense mass of dark green leaves, mostly 6 to 8 inches long. Twigs and smaller branches are as silvery gray as those of the Asian magnolias, but bark on larger branches is darker gray. Flowers are blue-green in bud and open yellowish green after the leaves have unfolded in late spring and so are mostly hidden.

Leaves of umbrella magnolia (*M. tripetala*), 10 to 20 inches long, form an umbrellalike canopy to heights of 20 feet in time. Native in much the same area as cucumbertree magnolia, this tree is equally hardy, growing reasonably well as far north as Ottawa, Canada, where annual minimum temperatures average −20°F or lower. Its flowers are creamy white, sometimes 10 inches across, opening in late spring. They are borne at the ends of branches and are very showy with the newly expanded leaves as background. Since the large, papery leaves are fragile, it is important to plant this tree in a protected site, a good idea for other magnolias as well.

Unlike many trees, magnolias are best transplanted in late spring, after new growth has started. They must be transplanted with a soil ball and should be moved to a large planting hole with the soil liberally amended with peat or well-rotted manure.

Magnolias are soft-wooded, and are sometimes damaged by ice storms. After broken branches have been pruned away, recovery is usually rapid unless the damage has been severe. Except for this problem, well-established magnolias usually give many years of service and beauty.

109

Hop-Hornbeam

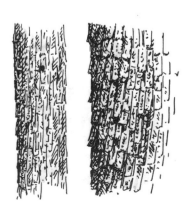

MANY POPULAR TREES ARE NATIVES that were introduced into landscape use as soon as their good qualities were known. Others have received only slow acceptance because of minor limitations that loomed large when they were first encountered. Hop-hornbeam (*Ostrya virginiana*), also called ironwood and leverwood, is a case in point. When this tree's limitations are understood they prove little hindrance to landscape use. The result is a beautiful and useful shade tree worthy of greater use.

The name hop-hornbeam refers to the inflated hoplike fruits, borne in hanging clusters 2 to 3 inches long. They are yellow-green at first and hardly noticeable among the leaves, but when fully inflated and nearly white in midsummer they offer considerable landscape interest.

The names hornbeam, ironwood, and leverwood refer to the extreme hardness of the wood. Tales of axes in the hands of unsuspecting novices bouncing off ironwood trunks have been told for many years by experienced woodsmen. This hard wood makes hop-hornbeam a durable tree. It is resistant to physical damage from ice and heavy snow, and reasonably long-lived.

Hop-hornbeam is sometimes confused with American hornbeam (*Carpinus caroliniana*), which is also called ironwood by some. Even though the two "ironwoods" are similar in many ways, they are easily sorted out by their bark. Hop-hornbeam has light gray-brown, vertically finely shredded bark that looks as if a cat may have used it for cleaning its claws. American hornbeam has smooth, light gray bark, more similar to that of beech.

110

Foliage of hop-hornbeam resembles that of birches and elms. The leaves are deep green and finely toothed, and usually turn bright yellow before falling. The close, vertically striated bark and handsomely molded trunks and limbs are interesting both before and after leaf-fall, but especially in spring, together with the delicate, lacy green new foliage.

This graceful member of the birch family, growing to 50 feet tall and occasionally taller, shows considerable variation in habit of growth. Some individuals are high-branching and gracefully vase-shaped, giving the effect of a small American elm. Others are more squat when grown in full sun, taking on more the shape of an open-grown beech. Such variations in form may not be apparent in woodland trees, elongated by the shady conditions, but can be seen after a few years in a nursery row.

Native to much of eastern North America, including some of the coldest climates of New England, New York, Michigan, and southern Minnesota, hop-hornbeam can be found growing on dry slopes, or sometimes even in rather wet soils, and is a fairly common species within its range. It is often seen in the open or on the edge of woodlands, but can also be found growing mostly under the shade of larger trees.

As this variety in natural habitats suggests, hop-hornbeam is widely adapted to sun or shade and dry or moist soil. But it has one serious limitation: very little tolerance of roadside salt. This removes it from consideration as a street tree in northern areas, but as a lawn shade tree it is most effective, casting dense enough shade for cooling but allowing enough light to penetrate the canopy to support lawn grasses underneath.

Hop-hornbeam is also useful in creating naturalized landscapes, where it can be planted partly in the shade of larger trees, or in the open. Opportunities often arise in landscape development to preserve existing trees, and this is a premium tree that should be earmarked for preservation whenever possible. The idea of saving specific trees *during* development is not offered as a substitute for preservation of natural woodlands *from* development, where that is appropriate, but rather as a way of conserving a useful landscape element when an entire plant association cannot be preserved.

Two traits of hop-hornbeam have limited its use. First, it has the reputation of being difficult to transplant. Skilled landscapers routinely do transplant it, however, and container-grown trees pose no problem even for amateurs. Second, it grows more slowly than some other trees, a disadvantage where quick landscape effect is needed. But as a general rule, slower-growing trees such as hop-hornbeam have denser, more durable wood than faster-growing species. When rapid growth is not essential, a little longer wait for this tree to reach functional size will be repaid handsomely by its durability.

Japanese Tree Lilac

FLOWERING TREES ALWAYS ARE AT A PREMIUM, especially in colder sections of the United States. One of the finest, even for these rigorous climates, is Japanese tree lilac. Truly a tree and yet truly a lilac, it flowers almost a month after most lilacs, and after most other flowering trees and shrubs, and then remains quietly attractive the rest of the year.

Japanese tree lilac (*Syringa reticulata,* also listed in catalogues as *Syringa amurensis* var. *japonica*) is native to Japan, as the name suggests. It has a less treelike variety, Amur lilac, that ranges northward through Manchuria to the Amur River region at the Siberian border. Japanese tree lilacs imported into the northeastern United States, whatever their origin in Asia, seem to be perfectly hardy, as evidenced by handsome old specimens growing in many places from northern New England to the Midwest.

Japanese tree lilac can be grown either as a single- or multiple-trunked tree or as a large screening shrub, depending on early pruning. In either case it will make a rounded to flat-topped specimen, sometimes as tall as 30 feet when grown as a tree. Its flowers appear in June, in only one color: creamy white. Flower clusters have a fuzzy appearance, unlike those of most lilacs, and in a good year will cover the canopy of the tree with bloom. As there are good years, so there must be not-so-good years, since this tree is an "alternate bloomer," flowering heavily every other year and only lightly in alternate years. When the flowers are fading and seeds are beginning to set, in June and July, microscopic flower buds are also being formed, to become the flowers of the next year. Since these simultaneous processes make considerable

112

demands on energy and food materials, they are in competition with each other, and seed-set takes precedence. If this year's flowering is light, sufficient energy and materials will be available for the initiation of a large number of flower buds for next year. But the resulting heavy seed-set next year will inhibit formation of new flower buds for the year following, and the result is a recurring pattern of alternating good and poor flowering years. The same phenomenon is seen in other trees and shrubs, and is responsible for the tendency toward alternate-year fruiting that has brought about the near-demise of certain older apple cultivars such as Northern Spy.

When planting young Japanese tree lilacs, resolve to be a little patient, since you may wait five to ten years for full flowering. Flowering may start on one side of the tree, or on a single branch, and alternate blooming will then perpetuate this one-sided flowering. To break the cycle so that the whole tree will flower next year, remove this year's flower clusters as soon as they wither. This prevents seed-set and conserves the plant's resources for development of flower buds for next year. Energetic gardeners can do this every year, to promote annual flowering, but as the tree grows larger the job of removing old flower clusters becomes time-consuming and impractical for most people.

Flowering is this tree's most colorful attribute, but it has other seasonal interest as well. Its fruits, if allowed to remain, turn from pale green to yellow and contrast with the dark green summer foliage. The leaves turn dull yellow and drop early in autumn, exposing deep reddish brown bark on trunk and branches. Horizontal lenticels in the bark give a lightly striped, cherrylike appearance that makes the tree interesting all winter.

Japanese tree lilac is not usually difficult to locate in nurseries in the Northeast, and is easy to transplant. It can be moved either in early spring or autumn in all but the coldest areas, where spring planting is less risky since it allows maximum time for new root growth before winter.

Once established, this tree grows well in any well-drained and reasonably fertile soil. Drainage is more important than fertility for all lilacs, but occasional fertilization of the soil may improve growth and flowering. When growing as a lawn specimen, this tree probably will receive all the fertilizer it needs from applications to the lawn. Liming of acid soils, long recommended for lilacs in general, may be a good thing, and certainly will do no harm, even though solid evidence in favor of the practice is scant.

Borers and scale insects may necessitate occasional timely spraying, but these problems are less common in the coldest climates than they are farther south. Given moderate care, Japanese tree lilac makes an effective flowering tree for even the most rigorous climates of the Northeast.

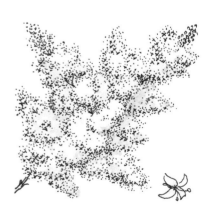

Korean Mountain Ash

CURIOUSLY, THE BEST LANDSCAPE TREE among the mountain ashes is one of the least known members of the group. Korean mountain ash (*Sorbus alnifolia*) differs from most of its relatives in several ways. It has simple rather than compound leaves (to the originator of the species name *alnifolia*, its simple leaves apparently resembled those of *Alnus*, or alder). It is a larger tree than most members of its group, eventually attaining a height of 50 feet. Its foliage becomes colorful in autumn. Last, but perhaps most important, it is more trouble free than most mountain ashes.

In his book, *Trees for American Gardens* (Macmillan, New York), Donald Wyman points out that, of more than thirty-five kinds of mountain ash planted in Boston's Arnold Arboretum, Korean mountain ash has been least troubled by borers. These pests seem to be less of a problem in northern than in southern New England, perhaps because extreme cold helps to control the overwintering borers. But in any area, when infestation does occur, a susceptible mountain ash tree can be virtually destroyed in a single growing season. Because of the seriousness of this problem, Korean mountain ash's relative freedom from these pests can be considered its greatest asset.

The more commonly used species—European (*Sorbus aucuparia*), American (*S. americana*), and showy (*S. decora*) mountain ashes—typically are used for accent, on a patio or in a corner of a backyard. Only occasionally do they become large enough to qualify as functional shade trees. Korean mountain ash, on the other hand, attains shade tree proportions with ease, old specimens sometimes reaching 50 feet in both height and spread. Because of its low branching, it is not a likely choice for street planting, but it is a fine moderate-sized lawn tree.

Northerners usually have a high regard for the seasons—not just spring or fall, but each season in turn; yet this is seldom reflected in the way we select landscape plants. Trees and shrubs often are chosen for their intense interest during a couple of weeks in spring, with little or no thought to their performance during the remainder of the year. Most of us are willing to devote a little space to the delicious but transient color and fragrance of lilacs, or to forsythia's brilliant heralding of spring, but for the bulk of our landscape plants, why not emphasize trees and shrubs that add color or interest during a major part of the year? Korean mountain ash is just such a tree.

Seasonal interest begins on the first clear day in January as the silvery gray twigs of this tree are sunlit against the blue winter sky. In spring, the branching pattern is accentuated by a growing mist of green, swelling buds. Flowers, among the largest found in the mountain ashes, open in late spring, along with those of native hawthorns. By this time, foliage is almost fully expanded and forms a crisply textured, green background for the white flowers. After the petals fall, the foliage remains dark green and healthy looking throughout summer, then turns to a rich golden orange in autumn. Meanwhile, fruits have been forming, turning clear red as they ripen in early autumn, then hanging on after the leaves have fallen. At this season, the tree can be spectacular with its silvery twigs and branches bearing a multitude of small, bright red fruits. Even though they are not so large as those of some of the other mountain ashes, they are well spaced in clusters, giving maximum color to the tree.

Korean mountain ash is hardy in areas with average annual minimum temperatures of −20°F to −25°F, once it is established. Because of its natural range through North Korea into Manchuria, with climates as severe as those of the coldest parts of the Northeast, it seems likely that trees from seed originating in such areas might be fully hardy throughout the northeastern United States. But there have been few opportunities to observe the performance of this tree in northern climates, and its precise limits of hardiness are yet to be established. Further trial by retail nurseries and residents of the North Country, with their necessity-borne willingness to experiment with untried plants, will tell the story. Meanwhile, the tree is available from a limited but growing number of both retail and wholesale nurseries. Any effort that may be required to locate it will be amply rewarded.

DECIDUOUS LARGE TREES
(48 feet and taller)
VIII

NOTHING DOES MORE TO MAKE A LANDSCAPE LIVABLE and esthetically pleasing than a large tree. In areas where old American elms still survive, they are most treasured for their cooling shade and comfortable feeling of overhead enclosure. Other trees may not give the same cathedral effect as American elm, but several can produce high shade and canopy, each in its own way. Those listed are among the best for northern areas but are not intended to form an exclusive list. Others that can be considered, at least for special situations, include other ashes, elms, and maples, cucumbertree magnolia, ginkgo, hickories (where existing natural stands can be preserved), and, for temporary effect, white and laurel willows, balsam poplar, and cottonwood.

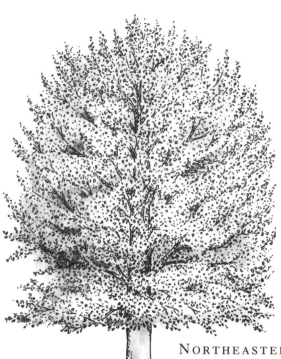

American Beech

NORTHEASTERN NORTH AMERICA is endowed with many beautiful native trees. One of the most impressive is the stately American beech (*Fagus grandifolia*), admired for its smooth, silvery gray bark, long-pointed winter buds, and deep green leaves which turn bronze or golden yellow in autumn. Fortunate residents of rural areas who are quick enough to arrive before the squirrels also enjoy its small but sweet nuts.

Few trees range as widely in eastern North American forests as beech. It is found from New Brunswick and Ontario southward to northern Florida and eastern Texas. In much of that area it shares with sugar maple the role of dominant tree of climax forests. Like all trees that grow wild over a wide range of latitude, beech is genetically variable in its response to climate. Best results can be expected in landscape plantings when trees from nearby seed sources are used, or at least when large differences between latitude of planting site and latitude of seed source are avoided. When northern seed sources are used, American beech is fully cold-hardy in areas where annual minimum temperatures average −25°F to −30°F, with occasional drops to −35°F or lower.

Under good growing conditions, American beech can reach a height of 100 feet. It will function well as a shade tree at heights of 30 to 50 feet, which it may reach in twenty to forty years, or sooner if large nursery-grown trees are planted. From the beginning it is a handsome tree in all seasons. Its striking silvery gray bark is accentuated by the lacy, light green spring foliage, which turns deep green by summer and golden bronze by midautumn. Flowers are hardly noticeable, but the small, angled nuts, borne singly or in pairs in small, prickly husks, add some interest in autumn, and both rodents and humans find them delicious. In winter, the glossy, spindle-shaped buds, about an inch long, are a distinctive feature.

American beech is at its best in soils that have good drainage but are adequately moist. When mature, its dense canopy of foliage and shallow roots discourage growth of turf grass underneath, and the simplest alternative is to cover the ground with a light mulch of bark or wood chips. The shallow root system is vulnerable to both physical damage and drought. Under no circumstance should vehicles be allowed to run over the ground close to beech trees, and it may be necessary to soak the ground occasionally during periods of dry weather.

In the northeastern United States and adjacent Canada, there are frequent opportunities to preserve beech trees, as well as other species, when land is being developed. That adds considerable landscape interest and real value to developed sites, but such attempts may be unsuccessful and costly if excavation is not done properly. American beech trees are easily destroyed when earth-moving equipment operates too close to tree trunks and runs over the feeding roots, which extend well beyond the spreading branches. Care must be taken to maintain plenty of free space around the trees both during and after construction.

Up until about twenty years ago, American beech had been generally trouble free, subject only to occasional outbreaks of scale insects, woolly aphids, and caterpillars, which could be controlled easily. But a more serious problem now exists: beech-bark disease, first diagnosed fifty years ago, has become destructive in the forests of the northeastern United States. To guard against the infection of landscape trees, it may be necessary in some areas to treat trees annually to control scale insects and thereby eliminate entry of the disease. Advice on this matter can be obtained from offices of the cooperative extension service, and treatment is best carried out by qualified arborists.

Transplanting beech trees is said to be difficult, but it really depends on the size and condition of the tree, the site, the skill with which transplanting is carried out, and the care provided afterward. Transplanting from the wild is risky, since it is difficult to move enough of the root system to supply the newly transplanted tree unless it's a very young seedling. Skilled plantsmen may succeed in moving small seedlings into a nursery to be grown to landscape size, but even that may be wasted effort for an amateur. Professional landscapers find that nursery-grown beech trees, with their shallow root systems, are easier to transplant successfully than tap-rooted trees. But the very nature of a shallow root system dictates that the tree be watered carefully for some time after transplanting. When that is done, the tree usually will recover fairly quickly and begin a lifetime of beauty and service.

Littleleaf Linden

IT IS ALMOST A TRUISM IN NORTHERN AREAS that native trees make the best and most reliable landscape trees. But there are many important exceptions to this rule. Europe's littleleaf linden (*Tilia cordata*) is one: it is fully as well adapted to cultivation here as our native linden or basswood (*Tilia americana*), and far more handsome and functional.

Lindens in considerable variety have graced European streets and parks for centuries. Of these, the little-leaf linden is the most widely adaptable and one of the most ornamental. As its name suggests, it has relatively small leaves (3 to 5 inches long), giving it a refined texture unusual among the lindens.

Lindens in general are not noted for strong seasonal color, and little-leaf linden is no exception. It is relatively slow to leaf out in spring—an advantage in climates known to have late spring freezes. When leaves do emerge, they are light green in color, typical of the newly emerging foliage of most trees. Small, creamy yellow flowers are then borne in clusters in early summer, when few other trees are in bloom. Like the flowers of most lindens, they are intensely attractive to honeybees. While not showy, they are interesting at close range (persons allergic to bee stings might better observe from a safe distance) and among the most fragrant of all tree flowers. The fruits that follow are small, round, and whitish yellow, conspicuous for the small leafy bracts attached to the fruiting stalks. From midsummer until autumn the foliage remains a uniform deep green on the upper surfaces, pale green below, with little color change before it falls. A word about autumn color: not every tree in the landscape must have it. Without quieter elements for contrast, showy foliage or flowers can cause multicolored confusion. Every landscape picture needs its background elements as well as its attention-getters.

Littleleaf linden is an outstanding city tree, but it is equally well suited to the country. It grows well in a variety of soils, tolerates occasional dryness or wetness, and is hardy in areas where winter temperatures reach −30°F in an average year, and −40°F on occasion. In fact, it is limited more in the Northeast by hot, dry summers than by cold winters. While it can be grown farther south, it is at its best in New England and the Great Lakes region.

Whether a tree is to be used in a street planting, or as a shade tree in a yard, the amount of maintenance it will require must be considered. Littleleaf linden is a low-maintenance tree. It is not particularly susceptible to damage from heavy ice and snow. It has no serious disease problems. Its small leaves present less of a litter problem than those of the larger-leaved lindens, and the sucker shoots that spring so readily from the bases of many linden trees are less of a problem with this species. On the other hand, leaf-chewing insects may disfigure the foliage in some years if the tree is not sprayed. This is about the only maintenance the tree requires, and it will succeed in spite of this occasional problem.

The typical form of littleleaf linden is more or less pyramidal, but varies greatly from tree to tree. There is much confusion about the growth rate that can be expected from this tree; it is often recommended as a small tree, yet reaches heights of 50 to 90 feet in time. One reason for the confusion is that individual trees vary greatly, not only in form but in growth rate as well. Selected trees with symmetrical form and fast growth have been propagated vegetatively, maintaining genetic identity in the offspring. Resulting groups of genetically identical individuals, called clones, then may be given horticultural variety names and grown and sold commercially. A noteworthy example is 'Greenspire,' a cultivar of littleleaf linden outstanding for its upright, pyramidal form and rapid growth. The original 'Greenspire' tree was selected from a cross between an outstanding tree found in a Boston park and a distinctively upright European variety.

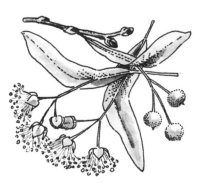

We prize many values in trees: fast growth, longevity, seasonal color, adaptability to different soils and climates, and resistance to insects, diseases, and storm breakage. No tree has all of these good qualities. No tree lacks all of them. For a widely adaptable tree with relatively little color but with few problems and good prospects for long life, consider littleleaf linden, the hardiest and best of the famous European lindens.

121

Norway Maple

NORWAY MAPLE (*Acer platanoides*) is a mixed blessing. Several traits put it far down the list of ideal shade trees. But its hardiness, rich deep green foliage, and early spring flowering interest insure it a place in at least some landscapes, provided it is used with full knowledge of its problems.

There are two main problems. First, Norway maple's heavy foliage casts such dense shade that turf grass and other ground cover plants underneath it have little chance of succeeding. This situation is made worse by its surface-feeding roots, which keep the soil around it too dry for those few ground cover plants that might tolerate the dense shade.

Of course, this is a problem only if one tries to grow vegetation under this tree. A better solution is simply to apply an attractive mulch. The mulched area can be separated from adjacent lawn by edging if neatness is a high priority. But remember that digging to insert edging will sever feeding roots even beyond the edge of the foliage canopy, possibly damaging the tree. If roots are encountered in digging, install a few feet of edging and leave further increments to be installed in succeeding years, allowing time for recovery before more cuts are made.

A potentially more serious problem is *Verticillium* wilt, a vascular disease caused by a fungus that lives in the soil. Severe infections are almost always fatal, but mild infections involving a small part of a tree have been overcome by fertilization with nitrogen. This is an uncertain control measure, but a good reason for regular fertilization of trees that are growing very slowly because of old age or a restricted root zone in city plantings.

122

Norway maple has good points as well. It is cold-hardy in all but the very coldest sections of the northeastern United States, in areas where annual minimum temperatures average close to −30°F, with occasional drops to −35°F or −40°F. Within its useful range, it tolerates city conditions better than most maples, and it is equally at home in rural areas.

Norway maple is one of the showiest of all maples in bloom, with greenish yellow flowers in clusters 2 inches or more across in early spring, contrasting with the dark gray-brown, evenly corrugated bark. Flowers appear a little later than the equally showy red ones of red maple, but before there is much other color in the landscape. The large leaves unfold quickly after the peak of flowering interest has passed, and form a dense, richly green mass that holds its color well into autumn. In years when severe freezes hold off until late autumn, the leaves of Norway maple may turn golden yellow before finally falling, but in the northeastern and north-central states this is the exception rather than the rule. When cold weather arrives on schedule, the leaves fall while still green.

Several selections have been made for form and foliage color. Not all are as cold-hardy as the species type, so it is a good idea to consult with local nurseries and others who have experience with the cultivar being considered.

'Columnare' is narrower than average, useful for areas where little lateral space is available. 'Erectum' is even more narrowly columnar, useful for vertical accent. 'Globosum' is broad-spreading but remains very low, seldom growing to more than 15 feet tall and resembling a large green lollipop—not a tree for informal or naturalized landscapes!

'Schwedleri,' the oldest red-leaved cultivar in use, gradually fades from rosy purple to bronze during the growing season, becoming deep green by late summer. 'Crimson King' and 'Royal Red' remain red-purple, almost black in fertile soil, through the leafy season. The red-leaved cultivars are slightly less cold-hardy than the species type, but withstand temperatures as low as −25°F while young and −30°F to −35°F when mature.

'Drummondii' or harlequin maple is one of the most distinctive of all maples, with strikingly white-variegated leaves. It is considerably slower growing than the species type, presumably because of the reduced chlorophyll-bearing leaf surface, and less cold-hardy, probably useful only where annual minimum temperatures average no lower than −15°F to −20°F.

All considered, Norway maple and its cultivars offer a broad range of function and landscape color. But if they are to perform satisfactorily, selection must be done with their problems as well as their assets in mind.

White Birches

RESIDENTS OF COLD CLIMATES who have to be content with a limited list of truly cold-hardy trees and shrubs, occasionally find compensations: landscape plants that perform well only in northern areas with cool summers. One of the most conspicuous of these is white or paper birch (*Betula papyrifera*), whose paper-white trunks make a dramatic year-round statement in the northern landscape.

Paper birch grows wild from Labrador to British Columbia and south to Pennsylvania and Nebraska, and performs well in cultivation through most of its native range. Landscapers attempt to use it in many areas south of this area, but usually it is short-lived at best. Ostensibly this is because of the ravages of the bronze birch borer, an insect that first enters high on the trunk, causing the top to die out. But the trouble begins before that, as trees are weakened by drought and high soil temperatures, becoming more susceptible to attack by borers.

It may be possible to avoid borer problems in some areas by selecting sites where the ground is shaded, and cooler than in nearby unshaded sites. One way is to plant on the shaded north sides of buildings. Another is to plant shrubs or ground cover plants for the shading effect their foliage has on the soil surface. When trees do not perform well in spite of such preferential treatment, it is more practical to try better-adapted species such as river birch (*Betula nigra*) than to take extreme measures to try to keep paper birch trees alive.

Where paper birch trees grow well, they will increase in height at a rate of more than a foot per year, ultimately reaching heights of 60 to 80 feet. The bark may remain amber or red-brown for ten years or more before turning papery white, but it is attractive even in the red-brown stage. Paper birch's graceful habit is impressive from youth to old age. Its deep green leaves are larger than those of some other birches and in autumn turn clear yellow before falling, making a colorful combination with the white trunks, and with the red foliage of other trees and shrubs. In early spring, the hanging, expanding catkins enhance the gracefulness of the tree.

Paper birch is often planted in clumps of three to five trunks, for accent, but single-trunked trees grow in height faster when shade is desired. Both single- and multiple-trunked trees can be found in nurseries. For successful transplanting, it is best to dig trees in early spring, or in autumn after the leaves have fallen. Transplanting a tree while it is growing usually dooms it to failure. No fertilizer should be added at planting, but light fertilization may be helpful once a newly planted tree is fully established.

Insect and disease problems other than borers are minor by comparison. But in some locations and years, leaf miners can disfigure the foliage, and carefully timed sprays may be necessary for protection. Instructions can be obtained from cooperative extension service offices.

Even though paper birch is the most impressive of the white-barked birches in its native territory, some of its close relatives are also popular. European white birch (*Betula pendula*) is similar to paper birch as a young tree, and its bark turns chalky white while it is very young, but usually it is shorter-lived. In any case it does not grow as tall as paper birch, topping off at 30 to 50 feet in most sites. Several cutleaved and weeping forms of European white birch are popular as specimen trees.

Gray birch (*Betula populifolia*), another short-lived tree, has conspicuous black markings on the bark. It is usually planted in clumps, for short-term accent. This small tree is likely to be bowed down or broken under ice and wet snow, and its foliage is often badly infested with leaf miners in the northeastern states. Other white-barked birches occasionally are available, but they have been used so little in the past that their performance is not fully predictable.

Paper birch is more cold-hardy than it needs to be to survive the low temperature extremes of the northeastern and north-central United States. European white birch is almost as cold-hardy, but some of the weeping cultivars may be damaged in the very coldest climates of the north-central states. Gray birch is less cold-hardy still, but useful where winter minimum temperatures do not fall below −25°F. Any of these trees will provide striking accent, but for long life and most impressive performance, paper birch is the best choice.

Red Maple

IT MAY BE TRUE THAT THERE IS NEITHER a faultless shade tree nor one without redeeming qualities. But that axiom, along with the value of diversity, accounts for the popularity of red or swamp maple (*Acer rubrum*). This tree lacks some of the elegance and longevity of sugar maple (*A. saccharum*) and is not so tolerant of difficult sites as the sometimes-weedy silver maple (*A. saccharinum*), but it combines fair durability with rather broad environmental tolerance, especially of wet soils, and it offers considerable seasonal color as well.

Red maple is unusually widely distributed in North America. It's found from Newfoundland to central Florida and westward over most of the eastern half of the United States. Although that makes for a large and useful range, it also creates problems. Trees from different range extremes are limited in cross-adaptability; at the very least, those of far southern origin should be avoided in far northern areas. That has become a practical problem with the introduction of new cultivars in recent years, because some have their origins in relatively mild climates and have failed in areas where winter temperatures reach −20°F and lower. The problem has been complicated in some cases by failure of graft unions, and many retail nurseries are adopting a wait-and-see attitude until the new cultivars are available on their own roots, propagated by cuttings.

Red maple seedlings can be transplanted from the wild, as is sometimes done by skilled nurserymen, who then grow them to landscape size in the nursery. For people without experience in transplanting, the cost in time and risk usually exceeds the cost of buying nursery-grown trees. Larger trees that have been dug from the woods and offered for sale without the benefit of a stay in the nursery for redevelopment of the root system are very risky indeed.

Because of its wide environmental tolerance, red maple is in demand for street as well as lawn plantings. It tolerates wet soils better than most other trees, but it will also grow in rather dry soils. It is adapted to the full range of soil acidity in eastern North America. Few sites are so exposed to sun and wind that red maple will not at least survive, but in extremely difficult sites, other trees, such as silver maple, may perform better.

The bright crimson flowers of red maple are small but borne in rather showy clusters in early spring. Trees with predominantly female flowers put on longer displays than do those with male flowers, because the red color is continued by the developing fruit. The difference is greatest in southern trees, but noticeable even in the Far North.

Red maple's greatest show of color comes in autumn, when the foliage turns shades of crimson to brilliant scarlet, coloring before most other trees. The smooth, silver-gray bark of branches and twigs complements the red flower and foliage colors in season, and provides interest in itself at other times.

Several cultivars of red maple selected for superior or unusual growth habit and outstanding autumn color have been introduced. 'Armstrong,' 'Bowhall,' and 'Columnare' are relatively narrow forms, and 'Globosum' and 'Tilford' are more or less globose in outline. 'Schlesingeri' and, more recently, 'Autumn Flame' have been selected for their unusually early autumn color. Other recent selections for outstanding autumn color include 'October Glory' and 'Red Sunset.' The last three have not been in use long enough for complete evaluation and may not prove adaptable to the coldest climates. In any case, you should consult experienced local nurserymen before trying new cultivars in any but a small or experimental way.

Growth rate and longevity of red maple are highly variable factors, depending on site conditions and differences among seedlings. Lawn trees grown with ample moisture will reach an attractive size in ten years or so and remain in good condition for several decades. But in dry soil or in street plantings, where little root space is available, growth may be only half as fast or less, and the useful life of trees may be no more than fifteen to twenty years.

The most serious problem of red maple is breakage from wind and ice storms. Even though red maple is not as weak-wooded as silver maple, its usefulness is limited in areas prone to frequent storms, especially ice storms. Several insects and diseases can affect this tree, but they are seldom serious enough to require control measures. Like other living organisms, however, insects and disease-agents are constantly changing, and new problems may arise. That is one of the best arguments against planting too many of any one kind of tree. Another caution about red maple: its leaves may be fatal to horses when ingested.

When all its limitations are considered, red maple still emerges as a useful landscape tree, especially because of its substantial landscape interest and its tolerance for poorly drained soils.

Red Oaks

OAK TREES ARE USUALLY CONSIDERED TO BE rugged and long-lived, but slow growing. Northern red oak (*Quercus rubra*, in the past called *Q. borealis*) and its relatives in the red oak group are indeed durable, but they are faster growing than their reputation suggests. These qualities make them popular shade trees for northern climates.

Trees in the red oak group have leaves with pointed, bristle-tipped lobes or, in a few cases, bristle-tipped leaves without lobes. This group includes about twenty temperate-zone species, many of them restricted to mild climates. But several species besides northern red oak are adapted to cold climates, including pin oak, shingle oak, scarlet oak, and black oak.

Northern red oak is the hardiest of the group. Trees from northern seed sources grow perfectly well in areas where annual minimum temperatures regularly reach −35°F and occasionally drop to −45°F or lower. Like most other oaks, this species is also tolerant of dry soils, succeeding as a street tree or a lawn shade tree, and it is the fastest-growing oak that can be used in northern areas. A tree five years old at planting can reach a height of 20 to 25 feet within ten to fifteen years. If the soil is reasonably good, it will eventually grow as tall as 70 feet with a spread of at least 40 feet. Its massive limbs have coarsely striped, light and dark gray bark, and its large leaves, with broad, sharp-pointed lobes, are lustrous and dark green, turning russet red in autumn.

A second member of the red oak group, pin oak (*Quercus palustris*), is also fast growing and is equally popular. It is different in form from northern red oak, with a straight, mastlike trunk and many slender side branches spreading laterally. The uppermost branches ascend and the lowest hang downward, sometimes to the ground. When this tree is used where space is limited, it may be necessary to remove a few lower branches to allow access underneath. Where sufficient space is available, the natural, fanlike, branching pattern is an attraction. It is better to apply a mulch around the base of an unpruned tree, rather than face the problem of mowing grass beneath the low-hanging branches.

In high-limestone soils—testing at pH 6.5 or higher—pin oak may suffer from lack of iron, causing the normally dark green, deeply cut leaves to become yellow, with reduced twig growth. Application of soluble iron to the foliage or soil can sometimes correct the situation. Directions can be obtained from cooperative extension service offices, but treatment of large trees is best left to qualified arborists, because of the equipment needed.

Pin oak is cold-hardy where annual minimum temperatures average −25°F, but cannot be relied on in the coldest parts of the Northeast and Midwest. A closely related and similar species, northern pin oak (*Quercus ellipsoidalis*), native in the northern Midwest to Manitoba, is more cold-hardy and can be substituted for *Q. palustris* in the Far North.

Shingle oak (*Quercus imbricaria*) is an especially interesting member of the red oak group. It has unlobed, dark green, leathery leaves that turn golden yellow or russet gold in autumn, then dry to a tan color and remain attached to the tree well into winter. The growth habit of shingle oak is similar to that of pin oak, and because it is tolerant of high-limestone soils, it is often substituted for pin oak in such soils. But shingle oak is slightly less cold-hardy than pin oak and should be used only experimentally where winter minimum temperatures regularly fall below −20°F.

Two other members of the red oak group are also useful in the North. Scarlet oak (*Quercus coccinea*) and black oak (*Quercus velutina*) are native to much of the eastern United States and will grow on very poor soil. Both are difficult to transplant and are not so widely available as red and pin oaks. The foliage of both is more deeply cut than that of red oak and turns bright crimson in autumn. Both are more irregular in growth habit than pin oak, are slower to attain functional size, and have a more open canopy; but they are similar to pin oak in cold-hardiness. Black and scarlet oak are not always available at nurseries, but if you have some on your land, they are worth preserving.

Trees in the red oak group cannot be counted on to live as long as some of the white oaks, but they usually do well for decades, and some will lend their beauty to the landscape for more than a hundred years.

Sugar Maple

NO RESIDENT OF THE NORTHEASTERN UNITED STATES needs to be told about sugar maple (*Acer saccharum*) and its value as a landscape tree. But a reminder about its limitations and requirements may be useful.

As used in northeastern landscapes, this native tree seems to pose a contradiction. It is known to be rugged, long-lived, and trouble free in many situations. Yet roadsides in late summer are marked by early-reddening leaves of sugar maples that are dying before their time. This apparent contradiction is easily explained: sugar maple is more susceptible to soil-related stresses than many other shade trees, including some other maples, but given favorable soil conditions it turns out to be one of the most satisfactory and trouble free of landscape trees.

What soil-related stresses prevent sugar maple from realizing its potential? One of the most important is poor aeration: the result of water-logging. Wet soils that would be tolerated by red and silver maples (*Acer rubrum* and *A. saccharinum*) can produce enough stress to kill sugar maple in a year or two. Flooding of soil has the effect of saturating normally air-filled soil pores with water. The result is too little soil oxygen to support normal root activity, and the absorption of water and other nutrients is hampered. This produces a situation in which too *much* water in the soil results in too *little* water in the living tissues at the top of the plant—a condition sometimes called "physiological drought."

When planting a tree in a spot where flooding is known to occur with any frequency, it may be possible to correct the situation in advance through grading or draining. If not, substitute for sugar maple a tree more tolerant of wet sites, such as red maple.

A second kind of soil-related stress is soil compaction, common at roadsides and construction sites. Compaction has the same general effect as flooding: reduced air-pore space in the soil. In addition, severe compaction, such as that caused by construction vehicles running over moist, soft soil beneath a tree, can physically shear off whole sections of the tree's feeding root systems. Remember that most of the effective root system is usually as far away from the trunk as the outer branch tips—20 to 30 feet or more from the trunk in the case of a mature sugar maple.

Damage from soil compaction during construction can be prevented by keeping construction vehicles well away from *all* trees that are to be preserved (not just sugar maples). This can be done by setting appropriate project limit lines, or by selecting contractors with a reputation for taking an interest in preserving trees during construction.

Another alleged cause of the decline and death of roadside sugar maples in the North is the heavy use of road de-icing salts. There is disagreement about how much roadside decline is attributable to these salts, but there is no question about the overall rigors of the highway environment. Sugar maples have graced New England back roads since those roads were first built, but modern highways produce new stresses. However these stresses are analyzed, it seems clear that sugar maples should not be planted close to major highways—if, in fact, any trees should be.

Just as sugar maples do not grow well in wet sites, neither do they grow well in very dry sites, and this is another reason for poor performance at roadside. But even though we agree that sugar maple is not a logical choice for roadside planting, it is a superb lawn and yard shade tree. Usually it is successful on suburban streets, provided that a reasonable volume of fertile, well-drained soil is available. Under favorable conditions, this tree will provide shade in summer, autumn foliage color, and a mist of tiny, pale yellow flowers in early spring, briefly conspicuous against a blue sky. In autumn, it will provide plenty of leaves to rake, pile, jump in, and add to the compost pile. In winter, it will be relatively resistant to breakage by ice and heavy snow, so it should require little maintenance, other than leaf raking, for many years.

With careful soil preparation before planting, occasional soaking of the soil during prolonged drought periods, and annual fertilization beginning a full year after planting (state and county cooperative extension service offices can supply detailed instructions), this usually rather slow-growing tree can be induced to reach functional size surprisingly soon. At that point, it proves an excellent investment in beauty, function, and property value.

White Ash

THE ADAGE THAT HASTE MAKES WASTE applies to tree growth as well as to human efforts at construction. Slow-growing trees, such as certain oaks and maples, usually have dense strong wood, and often outlive humans, providing comfort and usefulness to several generations. Fast-growing trees, such as poplars, willows, silver maple, Siberian elm, and tree-of-heaven, often are short-lived, weak-wooded, or both. But there are exceptions to this rule, and white ash (*Fraxinus americana*) is one of them. It is a fast-growing tree with considerable permanence—a satisfactory compromise between durability and the rapid attainment of functional size.

The true ash trees (*Fraxinus* species) belong to the olive family, along with such superficially unlikely kin as forsythia, lilac, privet, jasmine, and, of course, olive. More than sixty species of *Fraxinus* inhabit the north temperate zone and adjacent tropics. White ash is native to a large part of eastern North America, from Nova Scotia to Minnesota and southward to Florida and Texas. With such a large natural range, there is plenty of room for geographic variation. Wild trees resulting from generations of natural selection in northern Florida are well adapted to that region, but cannot be expected to succeed in Maine or Michigan. In the same way, trees of northern origin grow poorly in the Deep South. The wisdom of planting trees originating in comparable climates is obvious.

In addition to having broad climatic adaptability, individual trees show a wide tolerance of soil extremes, from acidic to neutral or slightly alkaline, and from poorly drained to occasionally droughty. But for consistently dry soils, there are better choices than white ash, among them the closely related green ash (*Fraxinus pennsylvanica*).

In good sites, white ash becomes a tall (to 100 feet), high-branched tree. Its leaves are compound, lustrous and dark green on top, light green or whitened underneath. As the chlorophyll fades in autumn, yellow pigments dominate the foliage. At about the same time, leaves take on an overlay of rosy purple, with some trees becoming very colorful in early autumn. This yellow-purple autumnal color combination can be seen in other members of the olive family: Japanese tree lilac, forsythia, Korean abelialeaf, and certain privets, for example.

Leaves fall before the end of autumn, leaving a pattern of stiffly upright twigs and branches, distinctive in appearance, but not a source of strong winter interest. Leafing-out starts rather late in spring, but once begun it is quickly completed.

Even though white ash has many good landscape qualities, it creates one serious problem. Large quantities of small but tough winged fruits (samaras) are borne on most trees, often in large clusters. They appear at the same time as, and at the expense of, maturation of foliage. The sapped leaves turn a dull yellowish or brownish green and fail to color well in autumn. Later, fallen fruiting clusters constitute a litter problem. If not raked up, the tough samaras will dull lawnmower blades quickly. Seeds that find a good place to germinate will turn up unexpectedly two or three years later as fast-growing weed seedlings.

Fortunately, "seedless" white ash trees are available for landscape use. The first non-fruiting selection, named 'Rosehill,' was selected in the Kansas City area in the 1960s. It has excellent foliage, turning rosy purple in autumn, and strong and symmetrical branching, but has shown some winter injury in southeastern South Dakota, where annual minimum temperatures average about −25°F. A second nonfruiting white ash, 'Autumn Purple,' was selected even more recently in Wisconsin and seems to be hardy in most of that state, which compares closely with all but the coldest parts of New England, with average annual minimum temperatures between −25°F and −30°F.

Considering its hardiness and fast growth in northern areas, 'Autumn Purple' seems to be the best nonfruiting selection at present for most of the North Country. It may not be the best, however, for milder climates, and in the South there may be better native selections than either of these. When it is not essential to use nonfruiting trees, individuals that are equal in other landscape qualities to the nonfruiting cultivars can be found growing wild in many areas. Other superior forms undoubtedly await discovery in the wild, and interest in developing even better ash cultivars surely will continue, considering the landscape value of this tree.

133

White Oaks

OAK TREES ARE SYMBOLS OF DURABILITY AND STRENGTH throughout much of the Northern Hemisphere. They usually live up to their reputation, adding long-lived majesty to both natural and planned landscapes.

At least seventy-five species of oak (*Quercus*) inhabit the north temperate zone, but relatively few are available for landscape use, and fewer still are both available and adapted to cold climates. Those commonly used in the northernmost United States and adjacent Canada can be divided into two groups—the red oaks and the white. Leaves of trees in the red oak group have pointed, bristle-tipped lobes; if they are without lobes, bristles can still be found at the leaf tips. Members of the white oak group have rounded lobes without bristles.

The white oak group includes more than twenty species, but the three most commonly planted in the North are white oak, swamp white oak, and bur oak. All three share the reputation of being slow growing, and this has limited their use. But with moderate fertilization and irrigation during prolonged drought, trees 5 feet tall at planting will often reach a height of 20 feet in twenty years. As they get older, their durability and longevity will more than compensate for their relatively slow rate of growth.

White oak (*Quercus alba*), an absolutely majestic tree, is native to most of the eastern United States, from Maine to Minnesota and south to Florida and Texas. Wide-spreading, massive limbs, covered with slightly shaggy, light gray bark, give old trees a distinctive character. At maturity, a tree 80 feet tall may also be 80 feet across the crown. Even young trees show a ruggedness that portends their future character. The bluish green, round-lobed leaves of white oak form a canopy dense enough to offer shade, but open and high enough to allow plenty of diffused light for plants below. In autumn the leaves turn purple, then russet, before falling. White oak is adapted to all but the very coldest parts of the northeastern states. It grows in areas where annual minimum temperatures average as low as $-25°F$ with occasional drops to $-35°F$ or $-40°F$.

Swamp white oak (*Quercus bicolor*) gets its botanical name from the whitened undersides of its lustrous, round-toothed to shallowly lobed leaves. Its common name comes from its natural occurrence in wet habitats. Although it will grow better than most oaks in wet soils, it does at least as well in well-drained soils.

The branches of swamp white oak do not spread so widely as those of white oak, but are just as rugged in appearance. This variety is among the easiest of oaks to transplant, and one of the most cold-hardy. Trees from northern seed sources grow well in areas with annual minimum temperatures averaging $-35°F$. Large trees can be found in Vermont's Northeast Kingdom, where temperatures of $-40°F$ or lower are recorded every few years.

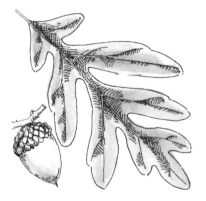

Bur oak (*Quercus macrocarpa*) is unusually well adapted for long-term survival, with the strong wood typical of the white oak group, very thick bark, deep roots, and unusually large acorns, protected and largely covered by a heavy cup. These features made it one of the few trees that could survive the dryness and periodic fires on the prairies.

The bur oak's corrugated bark, massive trunk and branches, and often thick and stubby side branches make it one of the easiest trees to recognize from a distance. Its lustrous, deep green leaves are variable in shape, with rounded teeth at the tip end and deeply cut, rounded lobes closer to the stem. The leaves show little color change in autumn.

Most temperate-zone trees have developed populations that are particularly well adapted to conditions in specific localities, but bur oak has carried this to unusual extremes. It naturally inhabits such climatically diverse areas as Nova Scotia, Manitoba, Tennessee, and Texas. Best results are usually obtained by planting trees grown from seeds that came from the same general part of the native range. Bur oak grows wild as a rather small tree in areas where annual minimum temperatures average close to $-40°F$, so it is hardy in the coldest parts of the northeastern and north-central United States.

All three of these white oaks are durable and free of serious problems, often surviving for 150 years and longer. All are functional shade trees and objects of great beauty. When one of them is planted, a gift is given to future generations. When one is saved from destruction during development of a piece of land, the gift is enjoyed by the present generation as well.

135

EVERGREEN
SHRUBS AND TREES

IX

EVERGREENS ARE AVAILABLE in all shrub and tree sizes. Their obvious advantage is that they retain their foliage mass throughout the year. This advantage is lost with very low evergreens that disappear from sight during winter in snowy climates, but tree evergreens can have a special charm when surrounded by snow.

Remember that evergreens are not inherently better or worse landscape plants than deciduous trees and shrubs. The choice should be based, as always, on the function for which the plant is needed. Remember also that variety makes things interesting. In most situations, a mixture of deciduous and evergreen shrubs and trees will have more appeal than a landscape that includes only evergreen, or only deciduous, plants.

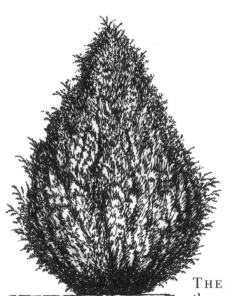

American Arborvitae

THE MOST COMMONLY USED EVERGREEN screening plant in the coldest parts of the northeastern United States is American arborvitae (*Thuja occidentalis*), also called white-cedar. This tall-growing shrub, sometimes a tree reaching heights of 50 feet or more, grows wild from Nova Scotia to Manitoba and southward to Illinois and the mountains of North Carolina. It is most often found growing in moist to wet soils, where it is at its best, but it can be used in sites with average soil moisture as well.

American arborvitae has dark green, scalelike leaves, bearing small glands that exude tiny drops of volatile "cedar" oil when the foliage is crushed. The foliage is the principal source of landscape interest, although the greenish brown cones, about half an inch long, add minor interest when they are borne in large numbers. Foliage of most plants turns brownish in winter, sometimes becoming decidedly unattractive. Fortunately, there are a few cultivars that hold their green color in winter well, especially 'Nigra' and 'Techny.'

American arborvitae and most of its cultivars are usefully hardy in the coldest parts of the northeastern states. But in areas where annual winter minimum temperatures average −25°F or lower, foliage may suffer some winter damage. Research at the University of Minnesota has shown that foliage injury seemingly caused by winter drying may actually be caused by fast freezing. On very cold, still, bright days, air temperatures may not rise much above zero Fahrenheit. Yet under these conditions foliage in full sun can be warmed to above freezing. When the sun then passes behind a building or is hidden by a cloud, the source of radiant heat is suddenly removed and the foliage cools to near air temperature in a minute or two, experiencing unusually rapid chilling. Such rapid freezing overcomes natural cellular defenses that protect tissues against injury from slower freezing to the same low temperatures.

The simplest way to prevent or reduce winter injury caused by fast freezing, in some situations, is to situate plants where they receive some shade from midday and afternoon sun in winter. Even the slight shade offered by leafless tree branches is sometimes enough.

American arborvitae will grow well in almost any soil that is not excessively dry. It is especially useful in wet, swampy soils, like those where it grows naturally, but is equally at home in soils of average moisture content. In really dry soils there are better choices, such as junipers. Even in moderately dry soils this plant may be damaged by mites, usually more troublesome when plants are under moisture stress.

In reasonably good soil, fertilization is not absolutely necessary, but light applications of a complete fertilizer every two or three years will help to keep plants full and vigorous, and may improve foliage color, especially in winter.

For best growth, this plant needs as much light as possible. It grows reasonably well when exposed to sun for only half the day, but fails miserably in full shade. When using arborvitae as a hedge, remember to shear it so that the bottom is wider than, or at least as wide as, the top, to allow better exposure to sun. Many hedges have failed to remain full at the base for this reason alone.

Even though American arborvitae is often used as a hedge or screen, its slower-growing cultivars make it more versatile than that. 'Douglasii Pyramidalis,' 'Hetz Wintergreen,' 'Nigra,' and 'Techny' are common tall-growing forms, fuller than the wild type and having better winter foliage color. These are excellent choices for screening but not appropriate for foundation plantings, where broader, lower-growing selections such as 'Wareana' and 'Woodwardii' remain in scale better. For really small-scale situations, 'Hetz Midget,' and 'Pumila' (Little Gem) grow only a few inches a year, remaining compact and in proportion for many years.

Transplanting of American arborvitae is best done as soon as summer's heat waves are over, in early autumn. New plantings should be watered thoroughly at planting and as necessary when the soil dries out during the first year. It is seldom necessary to irrigate established plants, if soils that dry out rapidly are avoided. Transplanting from the wild usually is not a good idea. Not only are wild plants more difficult to transplant successfully, but they seldom are as effective in the landscape as the better cultivars.

Pruning is seldom needed, except for hedges or to maintain greater fullness in screens. If it should be necessary, it is best done lightly to avoid leaving bare spots, and in early summer so that new growth will quickly cover the cut foliage.

With careful selection of soil and site, and a minimum of maintenance, American arborvitae is a reliable and functional landscape plant for cold climates in the Northeast.

Canada Hemlock

To perform well as a landscape plant, Canada hemlock (*Tsuga canadensis*) needs good soil and the right site. When these are provided, this evergreen develops a graceful form and rich green color unequalled by other native trees.

As its name suggests, it is a native of Canada, but the tree is indigenous to much of the northeastern United States as well. Its natural range extends from Nova Scotia and Minnesota southward to the mountains of northern Georgia and Alabama. In the Midwest, substantial stands of Canada hemlock in the northern Great Lakes region dwindle to small, isolated populations in Indiana and Illinois. The latter are scattered relics of the ice age, left behind in cool ravines and gorges as the last glacier receded, accompanied by climatic warming that left many areas too warm and dry for this species.

Ample soil moisture is an absolute requirement for Canada hemlock in landscape use as well as in natural stands. Hemlock trees planted in soils that experience severe summer drought may survive, but they will never grow well. Even when soil moisture is adequate, trees can dry out if they are exposed to sweeping winds, either in summer or winter. In exposed sites, more drought-resistant evergreens such as junipers or pines are better choices.

Canada hemlock is more broadly tolerant of light conditions than of wind, growing equally well in the North in full sun or considerable shade. In areas with hot, dry summers, it does best with at least some shade, performing well when planted on north sides of buildings.

140

Landscapers find Canada hemlock unusually versatile; it serves equally well as a specimen tree, a hedge, or in some situations a foundation plant. As a tree, it retains its lower branches for many years, given plenty of space. By the time the lower branches are finally gone, the trunk, covered with reddish bark, has become interesting and the form of the tree has developed a picturesque openness that gives it new character.

Canada hemlock has been used as a hedge plant for many years, and is one of the best of all evergreens for that purpose. In a good site, it can be established easily, as it transplants well and grows fairly rapidly. Inexpensive seedlings collected from the wild are often available within or near the species' native habitat, but fastest results can be obtained by starting with plants that have been growing in a nursery for at least a year or two.

When establishing a hemlock hedge, it is necessary to prune lightly and often during the first few years so the plants will fill out. Once established, hedges need to be pruned only once a year, in early summer. When a hedge is handled in this informal way, the basic shape is controlled by the annual shearing, while the feathery new growth restores some of the plant's natural gracefulness during the rest of the summer.

Use of Canada hemlock for foundation planting is common in some areas, but not always advisable. This tree normally grows to 75 feet or more, and it is difficult to hold it below window or even roof height. The most sensible way to keep hemlock trees small is to use dwarf or slow-growing specimens. Many such variants have been discovered in wild populations, and a number are available commercially—not in every nursery, but in a few, especially in the Northeast. Truly dwarf forms, some remaining under a few feet in height and width for many years, may be too slow growing for some uses, but they are valued for rock gardens and for small urban spaces. Specimens that are not truly dwarf but merely slow growing would eventually become quite large if left alone, but they need only a little pruning when used in foundation planting. Some of these forms are cultivars with their own names, while others are merely listed as "dwarf" or "slow growing." In either case, it is best to select individual plants at the nursery whenever possible.

One unusual form of Canada hemlock called 'Pendula,' the Sargent weeping hemlock, makes a striking accent plant in the garden. Its weeping branches and contorted trunks keep it below eye level for many years.

An array of diseases and insects can trouble hemlocks. Most are not often serious, provided the tree is growing in a good site with adequate moisture, but occasionally mites and scale insects become troublesome enough to require spraying. Otherwise, with minimal maintenance, this handsome native will perform well for many years.

Catawba Rhododendron

ON A VISIT to the Northeast Kingdom of Vermont, I was invited to view a Catawba rhododendron (*Rhododendron catawbiense*) planted by a friend several years earlier near the northeast corner of his home. Its foliage showed minimal signs of winterburn, and it was flowering profusely in early June. I remarked that perhaps the previous winter had been a mild one. My friend agreed, saying, "We had thirty-four degrees below zero around Christmas time, and I don't believe it got any colder than that all winter." That will give you an idea of what winter is like in the Northeast Kingdom, but it also makes the point that Catawba rhododendron, a native of the southern Appalachian mountains, is quite at home in many far northern areas.

Rhododendrons in general, as well as azaleas (also members of the genus *Rhododendron*) and other members of the Heath family (Ericaceae), including heathers, bearberry, blueberries, cranberries, and mountain laurel, have certain requirements in common. The most obvious is the need for acid soil, which nearly eliminates these plants from consideration in some areas. Even though acidity can be altered in some soils, general use of these plants is most practical where the soil is already below pH 5.5.

The plants also need well-drained but not excessively dry soil. There are exceptions: some azaleas and bog species grow well in wet soil, and a few, such as bearberry (*Arctostaphylos uva-ursi*), do well in dry, sandy soil. But most acid-soil plants share the general need for well-aerated soil with moderate moisture. One of the best ways to stabilize soil moisture is to spread an organic mulch and renew it every few years. This also reduces weed growth and stabilizes soil temperature.

After you've determined that your soil conditions are right for rhododendrons, you can deal with the question of cold-hardiness. A vast majority of the 600 or so species of *Rhododendron* are too tender for the colder climates of North America. Still, a considerable number of species are hardy, and these provide a broad spectrum of seasonal interest, with great variety in size and form, foliage texture and persistence, and

142

flower color and size. Among these, Catawba rhododendron is surely one of the most impressive, and it is hardy enough to grow in areas where the average annual minimum temperature is −30°F, with occasional drops to −40°F. But exposure to prevailing winds and afternoon sun in winter can cause injury by dehydration and rapid cooling of sun-heated foliage. In climates where minimum temperatures regularly drop below −20°F, the danger of such damage can be reduced by planting Catawba rhododendron on the north or east sides of the buildings, protected from late-day sun, and by using windbreaks to the north and west for protection from sweeping winds.

The landscape value of Catawba rhododendron is well known to anyone who has seen it in native stands in the Great Smoky Mountains. The leathery, evergreen leaves are elliptical, 3 to 5 inches long, forming a dense mass of neatly textured foliage at all times of the year. Mauve-purple flowers are borne in large clusters, blooming in early June in northern areas. Their color combines effectively with whites and yellows of other flowers. Flowering can be improved by cutting off blossoms as they wither to prevent fruit and seed from setting; otherwise, these will compete with formation of flower buds for the next year.

Mature Catawba rhododendrons seldom exceed 6 to 8 feet in height in native stands. In far northern areas they remain below eye level and can be massed or used individually as specimens or in foundation plantings. Their compact growth in cold climates makes the use of facing shrubs unnecessary, but hardy ground covers such as bearberry, lowbush blueberry (*Vaccinium angustifolium*), and mountain cranberry (*Vaccinium vitis-idaea*) are effective in combination.

Rhododendrons are susceptible to a variety of diseases and pests. Dieback diseases and root rot can be very serious, but are not likely to occur in new plantings. Leaf spots, mildew, and rust can be serious enough to require corrective treatment. Borers and weevils can cause severe damage and must be controlled when infestations occur. Rhododendrons should not be planted close to strawberries, because strawberry weevil is a major pest on both plants. Instructions for controlling diseases and insects can be obtained from state university or county cooperative extension service offices. Although you're not likely to have many problems at any one time, some difficulties may arise eventually, and you should take that into consideration when you select any rhododendron.

Many rhododendrons available in the North are hybrids of Catawba rhododendron. Most are not so hardy as the Catawba rhododendron itself, but some are nearly so. These so-called ironclad hybrids withstand average annual minimum temperatures of −10° to −15°F or lower, with occasional drops to −20°F or lower. Selected carefully and given the proper site conditions, Catawba rhododendron and its hybrids are excellent additions to the landscape.

Eastern
White Pine

THE STATELY BEAUTY of eastern white pine (*Pinus strobus*) is well known to those who live within the region of its natural distribution. Its climatic adaptability has led to its use outside its native range, as well. And its beauty and versatility have made it a favorite landscape tree wherever it can be used.

Eastern white pine grows wild from Nova Scotia to Minnesota and southward in the Appalachian Mountains to northern Georgia, and it is planted beyond the borders of its native range in the Midwest. As one would expect, wild trees that are the product of many generations of natural selection in the Far North acclimate themselves to winter earlier than their counterparts from the southern part of the range. But eastern white pine trees are not so tightly adapted to the climate of their origin as some other species. For example, trees originating in the southern Appalachians have been found to be climatically adapted to the lower Great Lakes region. In fact, they grow faster there than local stock.

As a young tree, eastern white pine grows upright with a symmetrical form, and its branches are usually close enough together to form a fair visual screen. Additional fullness can be induced by careful tip pruning in early summer while the new stem growth is immature. The soft, blue-green needles, in fascicles of five, are more slender than those of most other pines, giving the foliage a soft, airy appearance.

The symmetry so apparent in youth is gradually lost with age, and mature trees become more interesting in form, with open, layered branching. Old trees become flat-topped and picturesque, reaching heights of at least 80 feet in average landscape situations.

144

Eastern white pine will grow in almost any well-drained soil, but it is less tolerant of drought, wind, and roadside salt than pines with thicker needles, such as black or Austrian pine (*P. nigra*), red pine (*P. resinosa*), and Scots pine (*P. sylvestris*). So, reserve this excellent tree for better and more prominent sites, using coarser pines for roadsides, banks, and windbreaks.

Several unusual forms of eastern white pine are on the market, although they are not sold in every nursery. The narrowly upright selection 'Fastigiata' eventually becomes broad oval in outline. It is useful for vertical accent while young, or for screening where ground space is at a premium. Several dwarf or slow-growing selections, such as 'Nana' can be found in nurseries. Most are informally globular or pillowlike in form and are handsome and useful in small-scale plantings. The selection 'Pendula' has weeping branches and a main trunk that sends out a drooping shoot at the tip each year, keeping the entire plant low and pendulous. This striking plant is useful only for strong accent; it is too grotesque for some tastes.

Eastern white pine is not difficult to establish and maintain. Planting is best done either in spring or early enough in autumn to allow a long period of active root growth before the soil becomes too cold. Some "burning" of foliage may be seen the first winter after planting, but that is not a great problem as long as the buds are undamaged and new growth proceeds normally in spring. Little regular maintenance is needed other than careful pruning to encourage greater fullness in screen plantings.

The fungus that causes the most serious disease of this tree, white pine blister rust, must carry out part of its life cycle on certain currants and gooseberries (*Ribes* species). Most of those plants were once eradicated from areas where white pine is an important timber tree, but they have reestablished themselves in some places. Your county forester or cooperative extension service will be able to tell you if blister rust is a problem in your area. Obviously, one should not reintroduce currants, especially black currant (*Ribes nigrum*), or gooseberries, into areas where white pine is growing.

Insect problems usually are not serious, but it is wise to inspect white pine trees annually so that any infestations can be halted before insect populations can build up. The white pine weevil, an insect that kills the tree's central leader, can be a serious problem in timber stands, but usually not in landscape situations. Again, information on insect and disease problems and their control can be obtained from state and local cooperative extension service offices.

The popularity of eastern white pine as a landscape tree is a natural result of its beauty, versatility, and ability to succeed with minimum maintenance. It enhances its surroundings throughout its life, growing more beautiful through the years.

Firs

FAILURE OF LANDSCAPE PLANTS to survive extreme winters is discouraging to residents of the North Country, but there are compensations. Many areas having cold winters also have cool summers, and cool summers are the key to good performance for many landscape plants, including most of the true firs (*Abies* species).

The most common fir in landscape use is white fir (*Abies concolor*). This graceful tree has soft, blue-green, flattened and upward-curving needles, 1½ to 2 inches long. Individual trees vary in blueness, much like Colorado spruce. But blue Colorado spruce are so strong in color and formal in outline that they are objectionable in informal landscapes, where the bluest forms of white fir blend more readily.

Native to the southern Rocky Mountains, white fir is surprisingly well adapted to most of the northern United States. Seedlings from Colorado, probably the most cold-hardy available, are adaptable to areas with average annual minimum temperatures of −25°F and occasional drops to −35°F.

The waxy coating that gives the needles their bluish color also makes white fir more drought-tolerant than most firs. Even in the eastern Midwest, where summer heat and drought eliminate most firs from serious consideration, white fir performs surprisingly well.

146

This tree is most commonly used as a specimen, but it will also serve as a year-round visual screen for many years without pruning. Eventually, white firs shed their lower branches and lose their effectiveness for screening, but that can be forestalled for years by light fertilization of the trees and occasional thorough soaking of the soil during dry periods.

White fir responds well to annual shearing as a formal hedge, but plant-to-plant color variation may give the hedge a spotty look. As always in hedge pruning, leave the hedge wider at the base than at the top, exposing all of its surface to maximum sunlight.

The familiar balsam fir (*Abies balsamea*), native to the Northeast from Labrador to Minnesota, and its southern counterpart, Fraser fir (*Abies fraseri*), are important Christmas trees in much of the North, but seldom perform very well as landscape trees.

Several Asian firs are excellent landscape trees, but not all are sufficiently cold-hardy for far northern areas. Those from the coldest areas of Asia are so thoroughly adapted to short growing seasons that, like balsam fir, they break into rapid growth on the first warm days in spring, making them susceptible to late freezes. Other firs, from Japan and Korea, have more leisurely growth patterns, but are still quite cold-hardy. Three of the most widely tried in the northern United States are Korean fir (*Abies koreana*), Nikko fir (*A. homolepis*), and Veitch fir (*A. veitchii*).

Nikko and Veitch firs, both from Japan, have elegant foliage, much fuller than that of balsam fir. Their needles are glossy, dark green on top, much lighter underneath. Both of these firs function well for screening or as specimens in areas where annual winter temperatures average as low as −20°F, and perhaps in colder areas as well, if appropriate seed sources are selected.

Korean fir is a slow-growing tree, reaching a height of only about 20 feet after thirty years, and is seldom available commercially. But the handsome spreading form 'Prostrata' or 'Prostrate Beauty' shows great promise for northern landscapes, proving cold-hardy to at least −25°F. Its short, thick needles, densely clustered on the twig, are deep green on top and chalky white underneath, giving an interesting bicolored effect. Plants have grown to a height of 2 feet and a spread of 6 feet in fifteen years in Burlington, Vermont. Older plants in Boston have spread to 10 feet or more, while remaining only about 3 feet tall with the help of light pruning to remove an occasional vertical shoot that would allow the plant to revert to tree form. 'Prostrate Beauty,' which originated from cuttings taken from lower branches of a Korean fir tree, is easily repropagated for sale, but is not yet widely available.

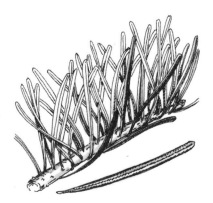

Whether there is a need for an evergreen screen, a specimen tree, or even a low shrub for massing or foundation planting, the firs offer foliage character seldom equalled by other evergreens.

Mountain Andromeda

MOUNTAIN ANDROMEDA (*Pieris floribunda*), a handsome evergreen shrub that flowers in early spring, is a highly functional landscape plant as well, adapted to most of New England and other areas of comparable climate and soils.

The generalization that broadleaved evergreens are most useful from the New England coast southward cannot be disputed. But generalization can be hazardous, because it ignores significant exceptions. There is a small but important group of broadleaved evergreens that can tolerate severe northern climates, if properly handled. Mountain andromeda is one of these. Even though it is native only as far north as the mountains of Virginia, its *useful range* extends throughout the Northeast and much of the Great Lakes region.

Both the common and scientific names of this plant suggest an association with Greek mythology. The name *Pieris* (from the Pierides, or Muses), was first given by an English botanist in the early nineteenth century, following the custom of that day of assigning names of Greek mythological figures to newly discovered plants. The common name suggests its similarity to the genus *Andromeda*—the shrubs named for the wife of Perseus by Carl von Linné (Linnaeus), Swedish botanist of the eighteenth century, considered to be the father of modern plant classification.

Even though mountain andromeda is a native of North America, it is less known and used here than its Asian relative, Japanese andromeda (*Pieris japonica*). The Japanese plant may be slightly more handsome than our native species, but this is not important in northern areas when the great difference in hardiness between the two is considered. Japanese andromeda is only fully hardy in areas with an average annual minimum temperature of −10°F or higher, even with careful attention to planting site. Mountain andromeda, on the other hand, is hardy to −30°F, as shown by tests conducted by the University of Vermont in the 1960s, at several sites in that state.

Mountain andromeda's landscape appeal is many-faceted. Its compact growth makes it useful for planting around small buildings and keeps its maximum height at 4 to 6 feet, the latter only in heavily shaded situations. Its lustrous, leathery, evergreen leaves are handsome throughout the winter. When spring finally arrives, this is one of the first shrubs to bloom, with profuse, waxy white flowers that resemble miniature lily-of-the-valley blossoms. They are borne in nodding, semi-erect clusters, in contrast to the pendulous flower clusters of Japanese andromeda.

Mountain andromeda is a member of the large and horticulturally impressive Heath family (Ericaceae), along with blueberries, rhododendrons, azaleas, and many bog and mountain-top plants. Members of this family are notoriously poor foragers for soil iron. Unlike many other plants, they do not have hair roots, with large absorptive surface areas. The usual function of hair roots is carried out by symbiotic associations of certain fungi with the plant roots. Since soil-inhabiting fungi grow best in acid conditions, and since availability of soil iron increases dramatically as the soil becomes more acid, these plants are able to absorb iron most easily in acid soil. This is why ericaceous plants often are referred to as "acid-soil plants" or "acid-loving plants."

Most broadleaved evergreens, including mountain andromeda, withstand northern winters best if not exposed to the full effects of winter sun and wind. Winter sun contributes to excessive drying of foliage, and causes harmful temperature fluctuations in plants. Its effects can be avoided simply by planting on the north or northeast sides of buildings, or other structures or plantings offering shade. Winter wind also causes excessive drying of foliage, at times when water cannot be replaced from frozen ground or through ice-plugged branches. The worst effects of wind can be avoided by planting within the shelter of windbreaks of hardier evergreens such as pines and spruces, by erecting fences for this purpose, or by taking advantage of existing microclimates around buildings or other structures. A simple way to locate such microclimates is to note leeward areas where snow collects in windy weather—but *not* areas where large amounts of snow fall from roofs or are deposited by snowplows.

Mountain andromeda can be transplanted with a soil ball in late spring or early autumn, or from containers at any time during the growing season. In the northern part of its useful range—northern New England, for example—it should be moved in spring (or in the early summer from containers), to allow plenty of time for root growth before winter. Once established, plants of mountain andromeda will add beauty to the landscape for many years.

149

Mountain Pines

SEVERAL PINES NATIVE TO MOUNTAINOUS AREAS in the Northern Hemisphere are useful landscape plants. All are slow growing compared with pines grown for timber—an advantage in many landscape situations—and adapted to use in lowlands as well as at high elevations. Three are of special interest to residents of cold climates.

The most common mountain pine in landscape use is Mugho pine (*Pinus mugo*), also called Swiss mountain pine or sometimes simply mountain pine. This shrubby plant from the Alps of Europe is so well adapted to northeastern North America that it has become naturalized in northern New Hampshire, and perhaps elsewhere.

Seedlings of Mugho pine vary widely in growth rate. Some individuals remain low and pillowlike for many years, while others stretch to heights of 10 feet in twenty years or less, usually becoming leggy and open at the base. Since this species is often placed close to one-story residences, it is important to estimate future growth before planting, selecting plants at a nursery when possible. Examination of stem growth made in recent seasons will give some idea of what to expect later on.

Even plants of the variety *mugo* (dwarf Mugho pine) are variable, although they remain lower and more dense than typical plants of the species. Dwarf clones, being propagated by a few nurseries, offer predictable growth rates, but are not yet available from very many retail sources.

The dark green needles of Mugho pine are only 1 to 3 inches long, borne in fascicles (clusters) of two. They usually persist on the twigs for four years, sometimes longer, giving the plant a luxuriant fullness that adds to its usefulness in forming low masses.

150

Several insect and disease problems can affect Mugho pine, but only one, pine needle scale, is a common problem. This insect can be controlled by carefully timed sprays applied by a specialist. The only other maintenance that is likely to be needed is pruning to control size, and this only when vigorous trees have been selected improperly for the small spaces in which they were planted.

Another native of the European Alps, and high elevations well into Asia, is Swiss stone pine (*Pinus cembra*). This handsome tree bears needles in fascicles of five, placing it in the white pine group along with our native eastern white pine (*Pinus strobus*). In form, Swiss stone pine is more similar to eastern white pine than to Mugho pine, but it grows much more slowly than eastern white pine and holds its needles twice as long, usually for four or five years. The result is that it forms a more dense foliage mass and is more formal in outline. Because of its slow growth it is an expensive tree to purchase, but in the long run its growth rate results in lower maintenance and replacement costs.

Swiss stone pine is an ideal evergreen for screening, but takes twenty years to grow tall enough. For similar results in less than half the time, eastern white pine is a better choice. But as a specimen for formal accent, Swiss stone pine is superb.

One of the most striking of all evergreens for formal accent is bristlecone pine (*Pinus aristata*). Wild trees growing on the western slopes of California's White Mountains have been widely publicized as the "world's oldest trees"; several have been found by radioactive carbon-dating to be more than 4,000 years old. While there is little resemblance between those gnarled giants and the slow-growing young specimens that have been planted in other areas, even small trees a few feet tall are distinctive in appearance, their plumy branches radiating in odd directions. Since this tree grows even more slowly than Swiss stone pine, it remains a shrubby specimen usually requiring at least a couple of decades to reach eye level.

Needles of bristlecone pine, in fascicles of five, are covered with natural white resin dots that can be mistaken for pine needle scale insects. These do no harm and are so small as to be inconspicuous except at very close range.

All three of these mountain pines are impressively cold-hardy. Mugho pine is adapted to the coldest climates in the United States, including localities where winter minimum temperatures average −40°F. The other two species have been used in so few areas that the full extent of their hardiness is not known. But conservatively, Swiss stone pine is adapted at least to −35°F, and bristlecone pine at least to −30°F.

Taken as a group, these three mountain pines offer impressive hardiness, long life, and a variety of functions. They are landscape plants for future as well as present generations.

Norway
Spruce

FEW NON-NATIVE CONIFERS are as widely accepted and as well adapted to landscape use in northeastern North America as Norway spruce (*Picea abies*). This major forest tree of northern Europe was introduced here in early Colonial times and has been widely used since as a windbreak and specimen tree.

Norway spruce becomes very tall in time, to at least 100 feet. When it is growing well it retains its lower branches with age, thereby occupying considerable ground area. Branches on the upper part of the tree ascend, while lower ones droop slightly. The main branches bear many strongly pendulous branchlets, giving them a distinctive fringelike appearance.

Foliage of Norway spruce is dark green and neatly textured, changing very little from summer to winter except when the lighter green new growth appears in late spring. Cones are deep tan and as much as 6 inches long, hanging conspicuously from upper branches of mature trees.

This evergreen is one of the most effective plants for year-round screens and windbreaks. It is adapted to the coldest climates of the northeastern United States and adjacent Canada, including areas where annual minimum temperatures average −35°F to −40°F, and sometimes dip lower still. It is not a good choice for the north-central plains of Minnesota, the Dakotas, and Manitoba, however, more because of drying winds than outright cold.

Norway spruce often remains trouble free for years, but is occasionally subject to destructive insect attacks, especially spruce budworm and spruce gall aphid. Control measures are available and should be used promptly and accurately when necessary. Information on pest control can be obtained from state and county cooperative extension service offices.

Even though Norway spruce is thought of first as a full-size tree, its slow-growing cultivars are among the most useful of evergreen shrubs. These range from truly dwarf plants that remain under 2 or 3 feet tall for many years to forms that are treelike but grow more slowly and develop a denser foliage mass than the species type.

Probably the most commonly used variant of Norway spruce is 'Nidiformis,' called nest spruce and actually resembling a bird's nest. This cultivar will remain under 3 feet in height for a couple of decades, with a spread close to half again its height. 'Maxwellii' (Maxwell spruce) has distinctly prickly foliage texture, but otherwise grows much the same as 'Nidiformis.' 'Procumbens' and 'Pumila' remain lower still, yet spread widely. Forms such as these are useful for doorway or foundation plantings in residential landscapes, or can be massed for low separation of outdoor areas.

Fully dwarf forms such as 'Gregoryana' and 'Pygmaea' remain below 18 inches in height for many years, and are useful in rock gardens or for accent in very small-scale plantings. Narrowly columnar variants such as 'Columnaris,' 'Cupressina,' and 'Pyramidata' are useful for screening where there is not enough ground space to accommodate the full-size species type.

The more dwarf a cultivar is, the more costly it is for nurseries to produce, primarily because of the slow growth but also because such variants do not reproduce true from seed but must be propagated by cuttings or grafts. As a result, the price may seem high in relation to the size of the plant being sold. Dwarf plants cost more originally, but savings in maintenance and replacement costs can make up the difference in a few years.

Another evergreen similar to Norway spruce in function, hardiness, and general landscape effect is white spruce (*Picea glauca*). This important timber tree, native to much of Canada and the northern United States, differs from Norway spruce in its smaller cones, more bluish green needles, and usually less pendulous branchlets. Norway spruce may be preferred for its richer dark green foliage, or white spruce simply because it is a native; otherwise the two can be considered to be interchangeable in landscape use.

Two variants of white spruce have found wide acceptance as landscape plants. 'Densata,' also called Black Hills spruce, is a slow-growing form originating in the Black Hills of South Dakota. This form is especially tolerant of the climate of the northern plains, making a very dense screen or windbreak that remains below 20 feet in height for many years. 'Conica,' also called dwarf Alberta spruce, is a dwarf, tightly conical juvenile dwarf that is susceptible to winterburn even where minimum temperatures do not usually fall to −15°F. It seldom grows faster than 2 inches annually, and specimens more than 6 or 8 feet tall are seldom seen.

Norway and white spruces and their variants grow well in most climates and soils of northeastern North America. They are a versatile group of evergreens for cold climates.

153

Yews

NO EVERGREEN IS MORE POPULAR in most of the northeastern United States than the yews (*Taxus* species). When well grown they are versatile landscape plants needing little care, and their foliage is handsome in all seasons.

Yews have succulent needles, dark green on the upper surfaces and pea green underneath, matching the color of fresh twigs. Flowers of only one sex are borne on an individual plant. Staminate (male) plants are noticeable in early summer when their flowers discharge large quantities of yellow pollen, and pistillate (female) plants are even more obvious when fruits mature later in the summer.

Fruits consist of dark brown seeds mostly enclosed in fleshy, red, cuplike arils. The seeds (but not the red arils) are poisonous if eaten, and so is the foliage, so it is a good idea not to plant yews where either plants or clippings from them will be accessible to livestock, and to teach children not to eat the "berries" (or those of any other unknown plant). Nonfruiting cultivars are usually available, but not always true-to-name.

Yews in cultivation in eastern North America are mostly clones or hybrids of Japanese yew (*Taxus cuspidata*). This native tree of Japan was introduced into the United States in 1861 as cuttings from low, spreading forms. For several years it was assumed that these showed the typical growth habit of the species, so when seedlings from wild trees were first grown in the eastern United States later in the nineteenth century, the name *capitata* was given to the upright, conical tree-form that resulted. This name is still used in many nurseries today. Since it is being applied to the wild species type it is botanically redundant, but it is so well entrenched in commerce that we probably shall see it for many years to come.

Whether we call this tree form *Taxus cuspidata* 'Capitata' (or *capitata*) or simply *T. cuspidata*, it is a useful evergreen, at its best when allowed to develop as a tree, eventually to 20 to 40 feet tall, its trunk displaying cinnamon brown or reddish brown bark. Too often this form is planted by foundations of houses. This works well for a few years, but eventually trees grow to a size where they must be pruned desperately to keep them in scale with their surroundings.

Many cultivars of Japanese yew have been selected, and some are truly superior landscape plants. Two of the best for the North are 'Nana' and 'Nigra.' 'Nana' is slow growing with an interesting "blocky" growth habit. Because of its slow growth it can be kept fairly small with little pruning, making it useful in small-scale landscapes. 'Nigra' is unusually dark green and retains its color well in winter. Both cultivars are hardy where annual minimum temperatures average −20°F to −25°F.

Another excellent selection, 'Densa,' is even more dwarf than 'Nana,' remaining below 3 to 4 feet for many years. Unfortunately, it is seldom available commercially, as its slow growth makes it costly for nurseries to produce and few consumers are willing to pay a price that would make it profitable. 'Densa' should not be confused with the similarly named cultivar 'Densiformis,' which is more tender in cold climates. Other good cultivars are available, best selected in consultation with local nurseries.

The much-photographed English and Irish yews (*Taxus baccata*) of the British Isles are, unfortunately, less cold-hardy than Japanese yews, performing well only where winter temperatures seldom fall below 0°F.

Hybrids between English and Japanese yews, collectively called Anglo-Japanese yews (*Taxus* x *media*), are variable in cold-hardiness and offer a variety of forms. Hatfield yew, a nonfruiting form reminiscent of Irish yew in its densely columnar form when young, is hardier than Irish yew, but still not useful where winter temperatures regularly drop much below −10°F. Two other Anglo-Japanese hybrids are similar in general form to Hatfield yew when young, and cold-hardy to −20°F. Of these, Hicks yew is a fruiting form, Stoveken yew nonfruiting.

Several Anglo-Japanese hybrids grow broader than tall, reaching a height of 8 to 10 feet and a spread of 15 to 20 feet or greater in time. One of these, Brown's yew, a nonfruiting form, is one of the hardiest of all Anglo-Japanese hybrids, withstanding low temperatures of −25°F. It is classified by some specialists as a selection of Japanese yew rather than a hybrid.

In selecting yews, first consider how cold-hardy they need to be, then whether upright or spreading cultivars are best suited to the spot where they are to be used. Sometimes it is possible to select further for fruiting or nonfruiting cultivars. Whichever cultivar is finally selected will provide year-round function and beauty.

155

Brooklyn Botanic Garden, Handbooks on gardening subjects, special printings of *Plants & Gardens*, Brooklyn Botanic Garden Record: 23. *Mulches*; 41. *Flowering Trees*; 47. *Dwarf Conifers*; 60. *Handbook on Conifers*; 65. *Tree and Shrub Forms—Their Landscape Use*; 66. *Rhododendrons and their Relatives*; 73. *Weed Control*; 83. *Nursery Source Guide*; 86. *Groundcovers and Vines*; 89. *Gardening without Pests*; 94. *Flowering Shrubs*; 95. *Pruning*. Brooklyn Botanic Garden, 1000 Washington Avenue, Brooklyn, N.Y. 11225.

Bush-Brown, James and Louise, *America's Garden Book*, New York: Scribner's, rev. ed., 1980.

Carr, Anna, *Rodale's Color Handbook of Garden Pests*, Emmaus, Pa. 18019: Rodale Press, 1979.

Cravens, Richard H., *Vines: Time-Life Encyclopedia of Gardening*, Alexandria, Va.: Time-Life Books, 1979.

Crockett, James Underwood, *Evergreens: Time-Life Encyclopedia of Gardening*, Alexandria, Va.: Time-Life Books, 1971.

———, *Flowering Shrubs: Time-Life Encyclopedia of Gardening*, Alexandria, Va.: Time-Life Books, 1972.

———, *Lawns and Groundcovers: Time-Life Encyclopedia of Gardening*, Alexandria, Va.: Time-Life Books, 1971.

———, *Trees: Time-Life Encyclopedia of Gardening*, Alexandria, Va.: Time-Life Books, 1972.

Flemer, William, III, *Nature's Guide to Successful Gardening and Landscaping*, New York: Crowell, 1972.

Flint, Harrison L., Landscape Plants for Eastern North America, New York: Wiley, 1983.

Foley, Daniel J., *Ground Covers for Easier Gardening*, Philadelphia: Chilton, 1961; repr. paperback, New York: Dover Publications, 1972.

Lape, Fred, *A Garden of Trees and Shrubs*, Ithaca, N.Y.: Cornell University Press, 1965.

Neely, Dan, and E. B. Himelick, *Fertilizing and Watering Trees*, Urbana, Ill.: Illinois Natural History Survey, Circular 52, 1971.

Pirone, P. P., *Diseases and Pests of Ornamental Plants*, New York: Wiley, 5th ed., 1978.

———, *Tree Maintenance*, New York: Oxford University Press, 4th ed., 1972.

Sherk, L. C., and A. R. Buckley, *Ornamental Shrubs for Canada*, Ottawa: Agriculture Canada, 1968.

Snyder, Leon C., *Trees and Shrubs for Northern Gardens*, Minneapolis: University of Minnesota Press, 1980.

Symonds, G. W. D., *The Shrub Identification Book*, New York: Barrows, 1963.

———, *The Tree Identification Book*, New York: Barrows, 1963.

Viertel, A. T., *Trees, Shrubs, and Vines: A Pictorial Guide to the Ornamental Woody Plants of the Northern United States, Exclusive of Conifers*, Syracuse, N.Y.: Syracuse University Press, 1970.

Wescott, Cynthia, *Wescott's Plant Disease Handbook*, New York: Van Nostrand, 4th ed., revised and edited by R. Kenneth Horst, 1979.

Wilson, Dan A., Thomas J. Wilson, and Wayne G. Tlusty, *Planning and Designing Your Home Landscape*, Madison: University of Wisconsin Extension Service, 1981.

Wyman, Donald, *Dwarf Shrubs, Maintenance-free Woody Plants for Today's Gardens*, New York: Macmillan, 1975.

———, *Ground Cover Plants*, New York: Macmillan, 1956.

———, *Shrubs and Vines for American Gardens*, New York: Macmillan, 2nd ed., 1969.

———, *Trees for American Gardens*, New York: Macmillan, 2nd. ed., 1965.

———, *Wyman's Garden Encyclopedia*, New York: Macmillan, 1971.

Selected
Bibliography

Index